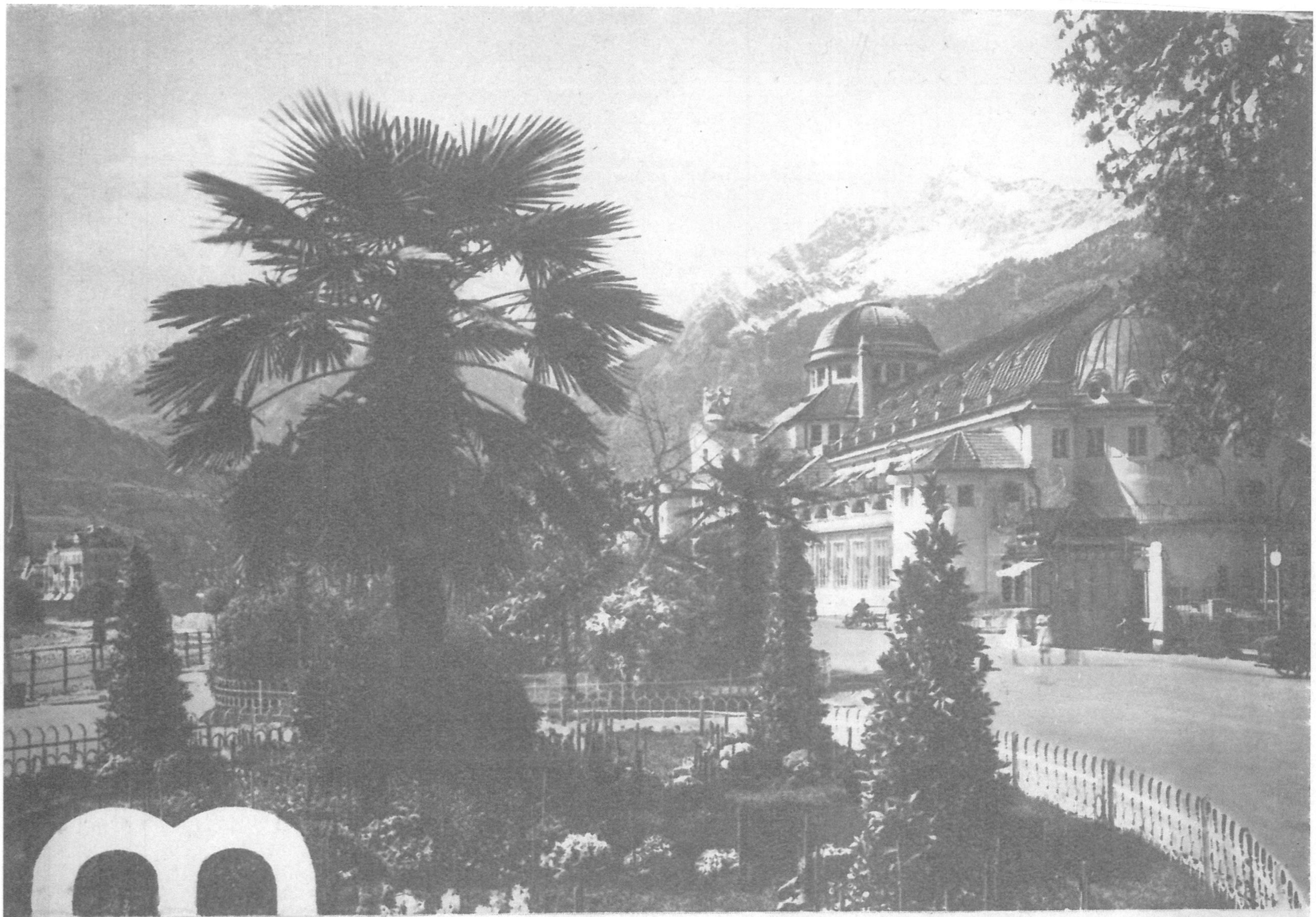

merano

LA STAGIONE ESTIVA
LA SAISON D'ÉTÉ
IN SUMMER
ZUR SOMMERZEIT

A peculiar phenomenon of the Alpine town
Merano is its large population of palm trees.
In parks and gardens, tall palm trees are to be
seen against a backdrop of snow-covered mountains. The majority of the palms belong to the
species *Trachycarpus fortunei*, which was brought
to Europe from East Asia in the 1830s. The first
palms were planted in Merano around 1880 as
the town was transforming into a thermal health
resort and a tourist destination. With this publi-
cation, I seek to trace the palm trees' botanical
trajectories and symbolic dimensions.

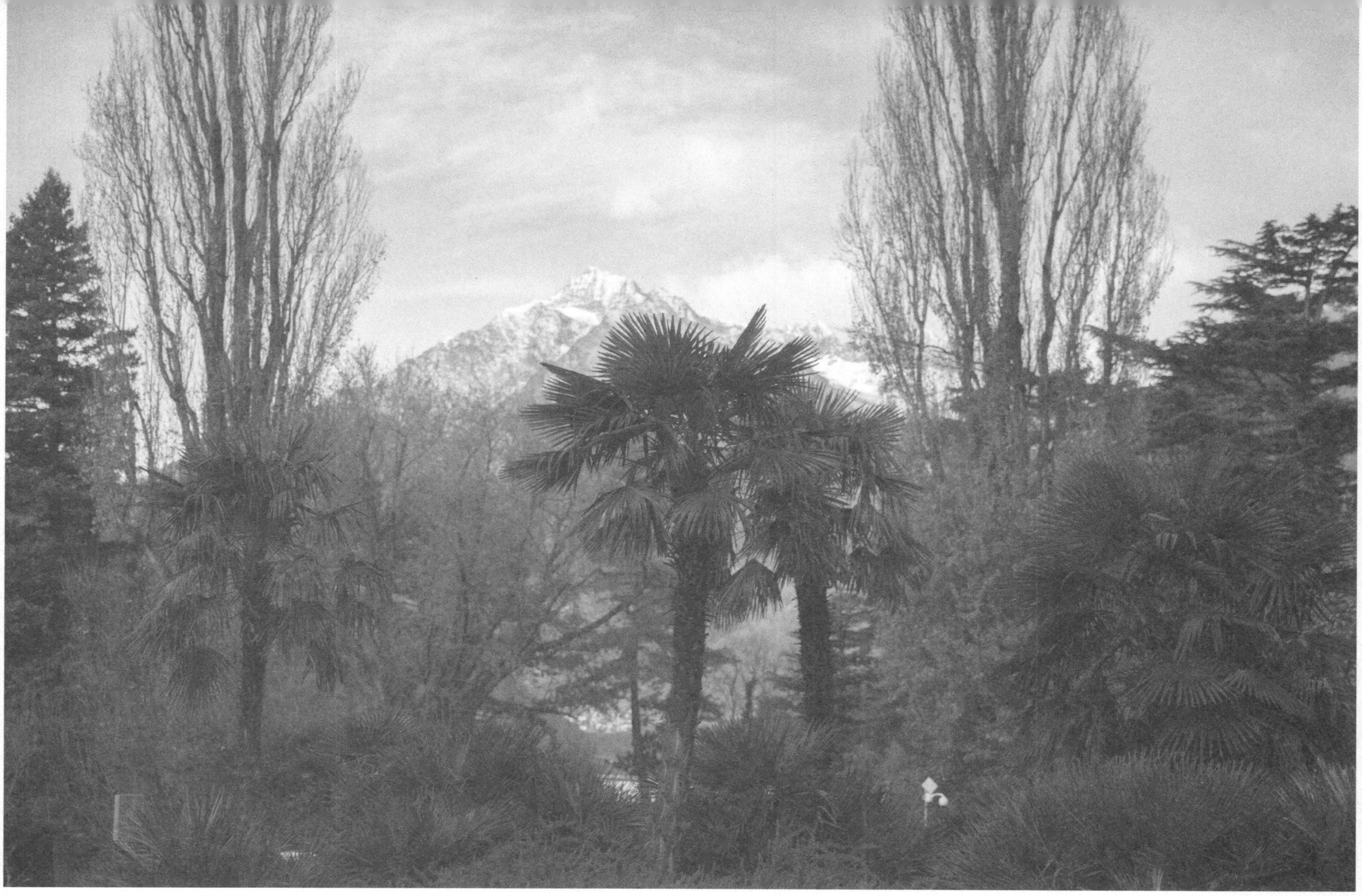

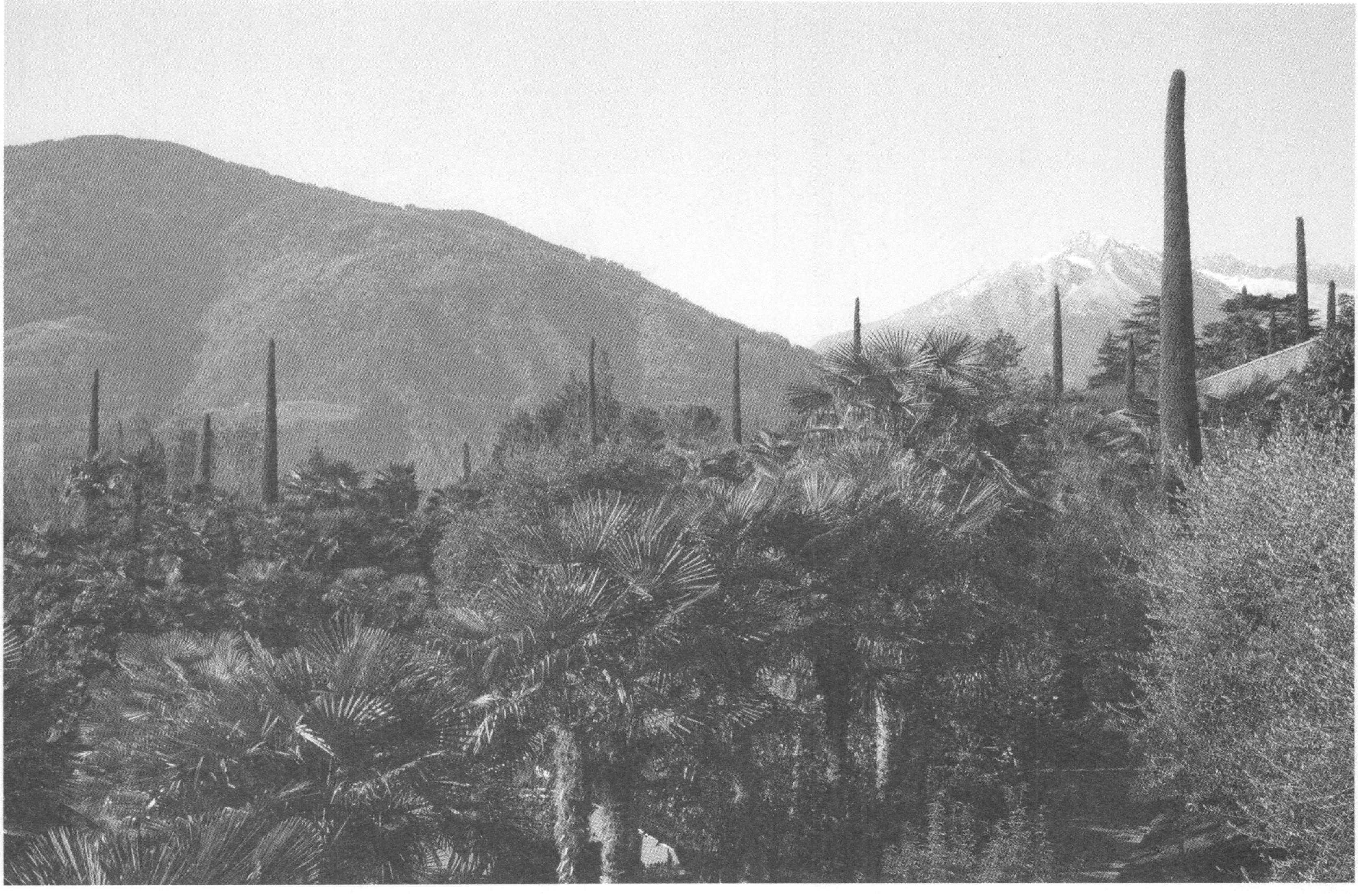

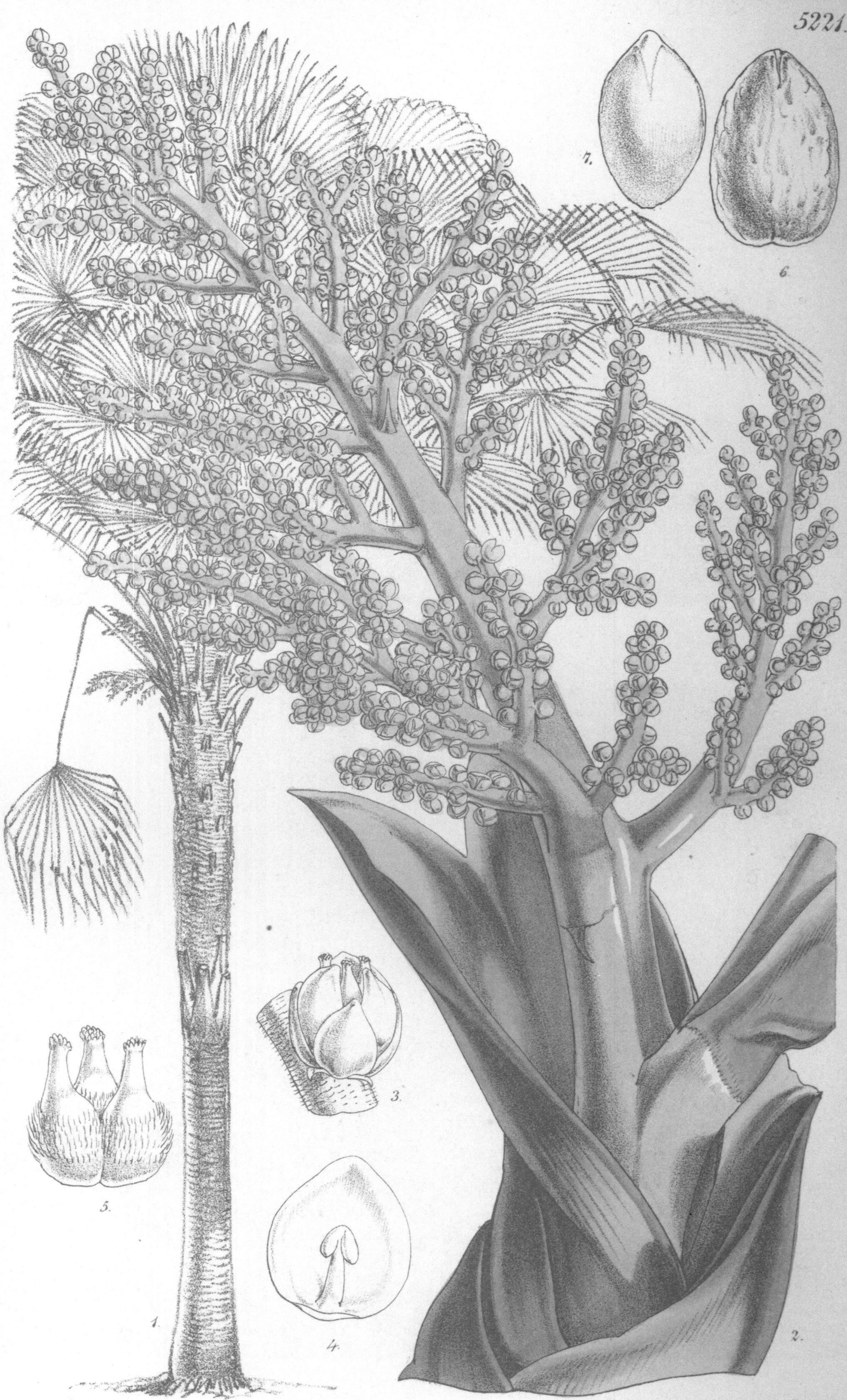

W. Fitch, del et lith.

Vincent Brooks Imp

The *Trachycarpus fortunei* is a slow-growing mountain palm.

Its common names are Chusan palm and Chinese windmill palm.

The palm thrives in temperate zones, but is unhappy in the tropics.

It is extremely resistant to cold, frost, and snow.

It has dark-green fan-shaped leaves.

Brown fibers cover the tree trunk. Their dark color attracts the warmth of sunlight.

A coarse green wax covers the leaves and stems, which makes the tree cold hardy.

The flowers are yellow (male) and greenish (female).

The fruits are small with rough exteriors. They are generally black when mature.

The seeds germinate easily within a few weeks of sowing.

The palm's trunk fibers are used for brushes, brooms, rope, and sacks.

Its seeds are used medicinally and are believed to have anticancer properties.

The species is widely cultivated as an ornamental plant, especially in colder climates.

The palm can live up to 150 years of age and grow to a height of more than 12 meters.

It tends to sulk in the summer, waiting for cooler weather in which to grow.

Growth is fastest at night.

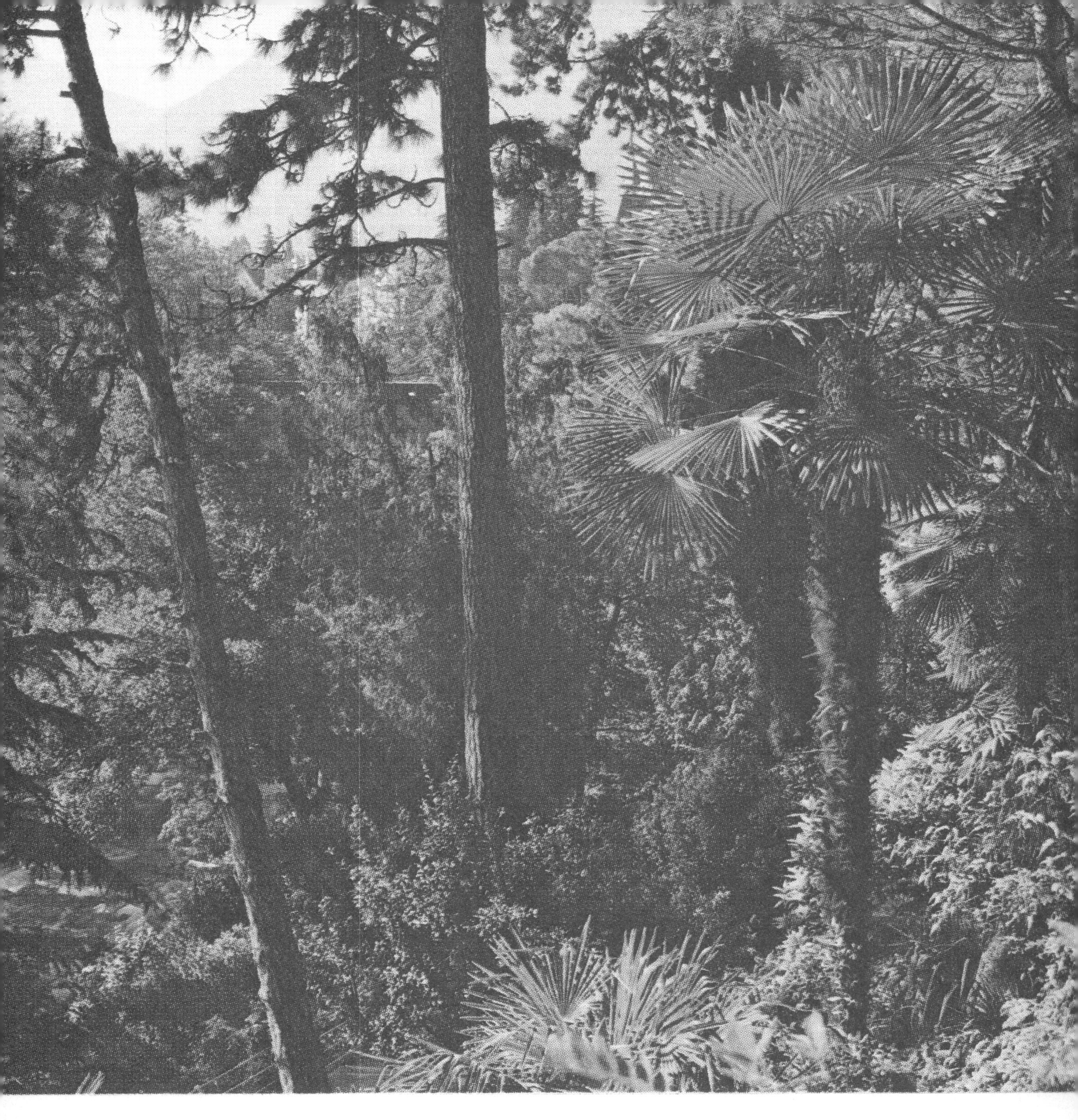

Tropische Vegetation in der Gilfanlage.

70 Schwarzkiefer. Mitte: Gelbkiefer. Rechts: Japanische Hanfpalme.

The *Trachycarpus fortunei* is thought to be indigenous to Eastern China.

The German physician Philipp Franz von Siebold brought the first seeds of the species from Japan to Europe in 1830.

However, it was the Scottish botanist Robert Fortune who was responsible for a successful introduction of the species some 20 years later.

He first saw the palm on the island of Chusan off the coast of East China. Disguised as "a Chinese from a distant province," he gathered seeds that were sent to the Royal Botanic Gardens in Kew, England.

The *Trachycarpus fortunei* was introduced to Merano around 1880, along with other foreign plant species.

The Merano palm trees are mentioned for the first time in Dr. A. F. Entleutner's book, *Eine Promenade durch die Anlagen und Gärten des climatischen Curortes Meran* (1886).

The palms he mentions were located in the garden of the then Maur Castle (today the Palace Hotel). They are described as *Chamaerops excelsa*, an earlier name for the *Trachycarpus fortunei*.

In the local archives, no traces are to be found of who planted these first palms.

In old photographs, it appears that the young palm trees were covered during winter. Years later, it was found that the palms didn't need the winter protection.

With palm trees and snow-capped mountains, Merano has been promoted as a spa resort since the late 19th century.

Today, palm seeds can be bought from dispensers along local walking trails. Meanwhile, the *Trachycarpus fortunei* is considered an invasive species in nearby regions, and some Merano gardeners see it as a weed.

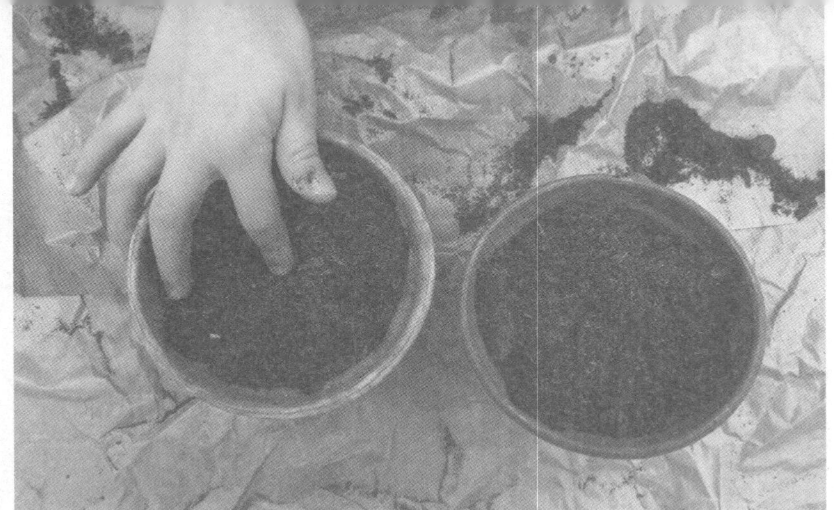

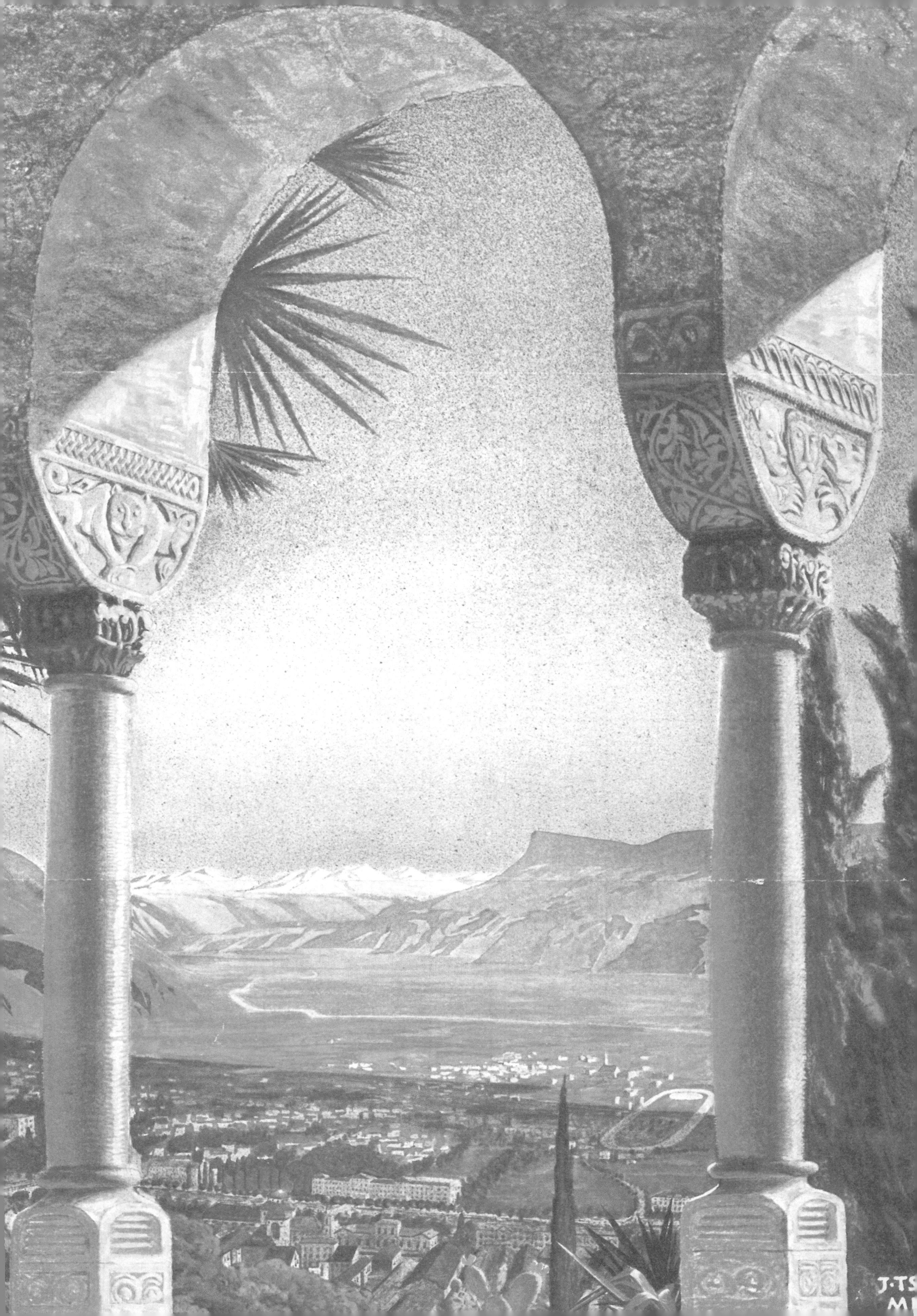
J·TS·
M

PALMATE LEAVES

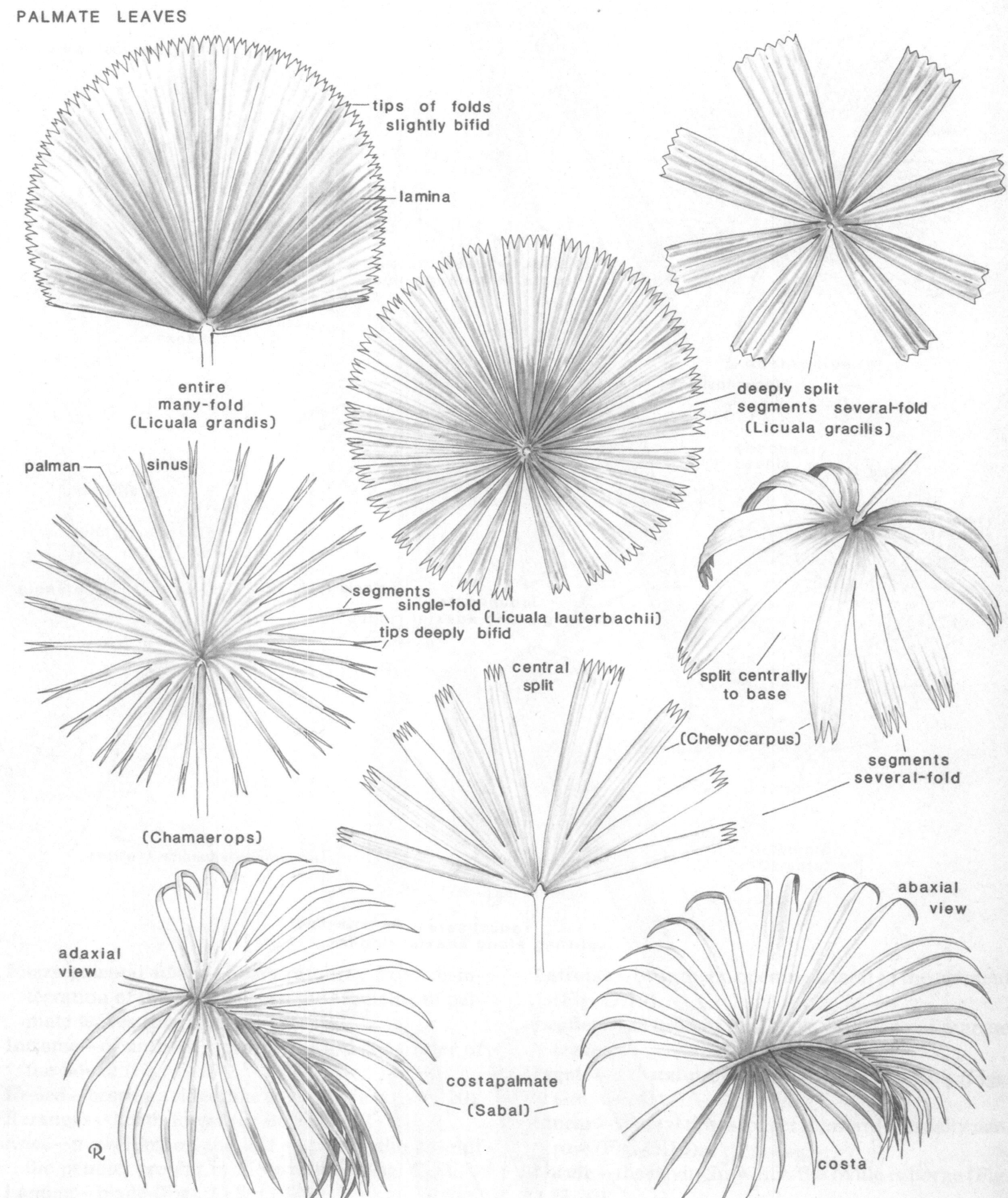

G.10—Palmate Leaves.

Trajectories of the Trachycarpus Fortunei

A conversation with Merano-based ecologist and botanist Otto Huber, author of *Die Botanik in Südtirol* (2012).

Nanna Debois Buhl: I am interested in the layers of stories and histories related to a given site, and I often investigate a place through its botany, animal life, and architecture. I am currently studying the peculiar phenomenon of palm trees in Merano, and I would like to talk to you about their trajectories. But firstly, what is your relationship to the flora of the region?

Otto Huber: I grew up here in South Tyrol and consider myself a Meraner. The South Tyrolean botany has become of increasing interest upon my return to this region after living 40 years abroad and focusing on tropical ecology.

NDB: Do you know when and how the first palms arrived to Merano?

OH: The Merano palm trees are primarily of the species *Trachycarpus fortunei*. Supposedly, the first palms were planted around 1880 in the garden of the Maur Castle in downtown Merano. It is unknown who planted them. Their existence is first mentioned in a book by Dr. A. F. Entleutner in 1886. There is plenty of literature on South Tyrolean botany in general, but very little on the palm trees in particular, in spite of the fact that they have been an important part of Merano's garden landscape since the turn of the 20th century.

NDB: Why does the *Trachycarpus fortunei* thrive so well in the climate of South Tyrol?

OH: In China, the *Trachycarpus fortunei* grows in the Himalayas. It thrives well in a temperate mountain climate and is one of the world's cold hardiest palms. Due to its hardiness, it has become very popular, not only in Southern Tyrol but also in other areas of Europe. In southern Italy, there are other palms native of the Mediterranean flora such as the *Chamaerops humilis*, but the *Trachycarpus fortunei* is the only palm species that we have in this region.

Merano is located in the only Alpine valley with a direct connection to the Mediterranean: our Adige valley stretches straight out south into the Po plain. Therefore, we have a unique combination of Mediterranean climate and snow-covered mountains.

NDB: On tourist advertising, Merano is often promoted through images of palm trees and snow-capped mountains. Apparently, the palm trees were used to attract the tourists from Northern Europe and the snowy mountain tops the tourists from the South. Do you think that Merano's palm trees are related to the city's establishment as a tourist destination?

OH: Yes, the connection is the following: in the early 1800s Merano was a small, insignificant town. It became known for its clean air and mild climate when Dr. Franz Tappeiner, an Austrian doctor, botanist, and anthropologist, settled here around 1850 to treat patients with respiratory disorders. The town became increasingly popular as a spa resort, especially when Sisi, the Empress Elisabeth of Austria, started paying frequent visits to the city. By the late 19th century, tourism was flourishing. A *Kurhaus* (or spa center) was established along with promenades, boulevards, and Grand Hotels. There was even a daily train connection to Vienna.

By then, Merano had turned into a garden city. Plenty of foreign plants were planted in the gardens of the villas and hotels. The Viennese upper class bought castles here and brought exotic plants to create the most impressive gardens. They might have been the ones who brought the first palms. From my window I see several castles, whose gardens have primarily introduced species: Lebanese cedars and North American pines. They were imported together with the palms and other exotic plants in the late 19th century.

NDB: What prompted this vogue for foreign plants?

OH: In Merano, a "leisure time flora" was created. In contrast to local utility plants, exotic species like the palms served as mere decoration. They signaled "luxury" and "faraway places." The use of hardy palms and other "exotic" plants in the temperate garden really owes its origins to European botanical expeditions of the 18th and 19th century, and to the Victorian passion for botany and plant collecting. There was a competition between the large botanical gardens in Europe to have the most exotic species. The botanic gardens in Kew (England) and Leiden (The Netherlands) were leading institutions. They sent their gardeners to the tropical and subtropical world to bring home interesting plants. It all started with the Prussian geographer and naturalist Alexander von Humboldt. Based on his extensive travels in Latin America around 1800, he was the first to scientifically describe the world of plants.

NDB: Do you think the palm trees have a different symbolic meaning for the inhabitants of Merano today than in the 1880s, when they were first introduced?

OH: Yes, because prior to their planting in local parks and gardens in the 1880s, most native people of Merano had never seen a palm before. Today, you see palm trees at every corner of the city. They have become part of the landscape.

NDB: I think the question of belonging is particularly interesting in border regions like this, which has had different national affiliations (the region belonged to Austria-Hungary until World War I) and still today has a bilingual population. I heard about a local dispute related to a new construction at a site where some old palm trees grow. While one party advocated for keeping the palm trees there, the other claimed that they could be removed because they don't belong to the local flora.

OH: In nearby regions, the *Trachycarpus fortunei* is considered an invasive species. In Merano, we currently experience an unexpected amount of palm seedlings. Botanical research is being conducted about how invasive the palm is here and whether it represents a danger to the native fauna, which I find unlikely.

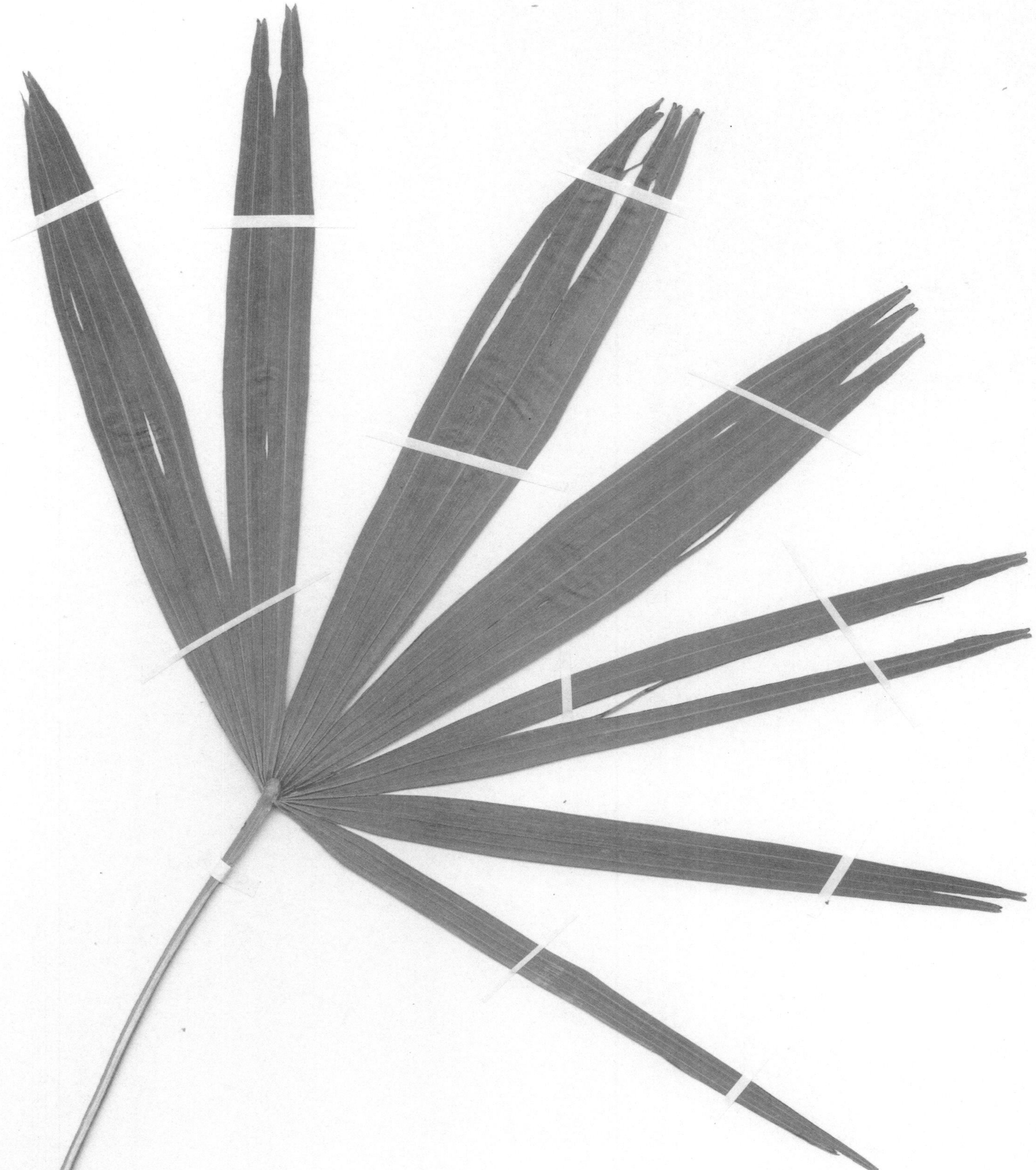

Trachycarpus.

(Hook.fil.)Wendl.
Trachycarpus fortunei.
Italien: Riva, kult.
8 . 7 . 1965.
H. Skovgaard Christensen

Ancac.

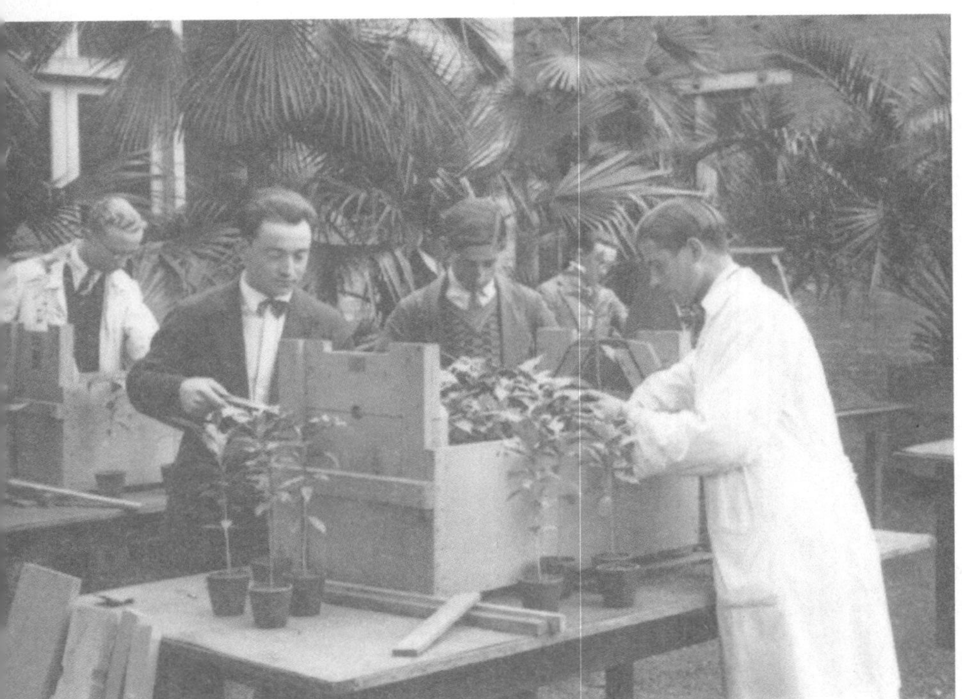

Eine Promenade

durch die

Anlagen und Gärten

des

climatischen Curortes Meran.

Von

Prof. Dr. A. F. Entleutner

Mitglied der k. k. zoologisch-botanischen Gesellschaft zu Wien,
der deutschen botan. Gesellschaft in Berlin, des naturhistor. Vereins
in Augsburg, des thüring. betan. Vereins „Irmischia" etc.

Meran 1886
S. Pötzelberger's Buchhandlung
(F. W. Ellmenreich).

Von hier gehen wir hinauf zu dem

Garten vom Schloss Mauer.

In diesem Garten ist unsere grösste Zwergpalme (Chamaerops excelsa Thb.), welche vor 7 Jahren gepflanzt wurde und im Jahre 1884 bei einer Höhe von ca. $3^1/_2$ m zum ersten Mal geblüht hat.

Daneben ist Darwin's Sauerdorn (Berberis Darwini Hook.) aus Chili und Patagonien. Ein immergrüner Strauch, dessen junge Aeste flaumhaarig sind. Seine lederartigen, mit stechenden Sägezähnen versehenen Blätter sind oberseits dunkel-, unterseits hellgrün. Die glänzend orangefarbenen Blüthen erscheinen an rothen Stielen in nickenden Doldentrauben. Die blaugrünlich - schwärzlichen Beeren sind flaschenförmig.

Oestlich vom Bassin, von Rosen umgeben, steht eine Torano-Fichte (Abies polita S. et Z.) aus Japan mit ringsherum stehenden, etwas nach oben gekrümmten, viereckigen, dicken Nadeln, die in eine stechende Spitze auslaufen. Diese schöne Fichte mit kastanienbraunen Zapfen wird in ihrer Heimath 40 m hoch und zeichnet sich durch ihre hellgrüne Färbung aus.

Die kanadische Hemlockstanne, Schierlings-Tanne (Tsuga canadensis Carr.).

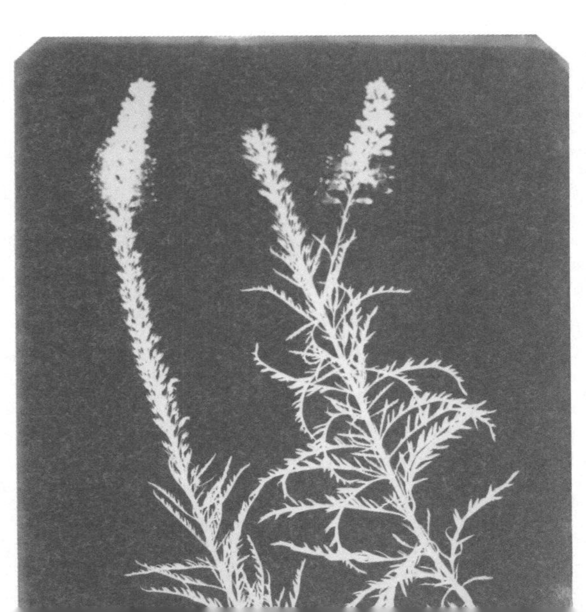

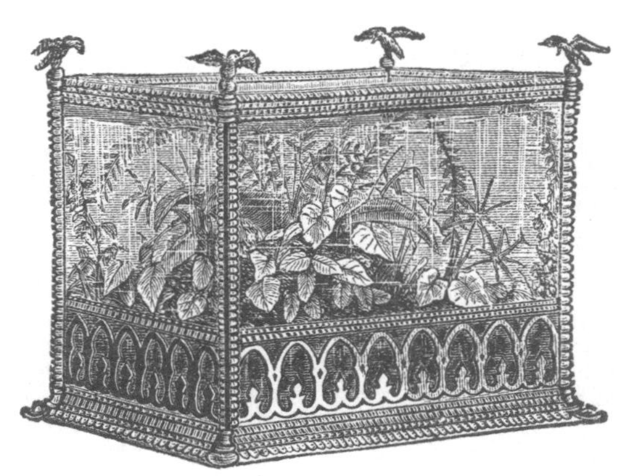

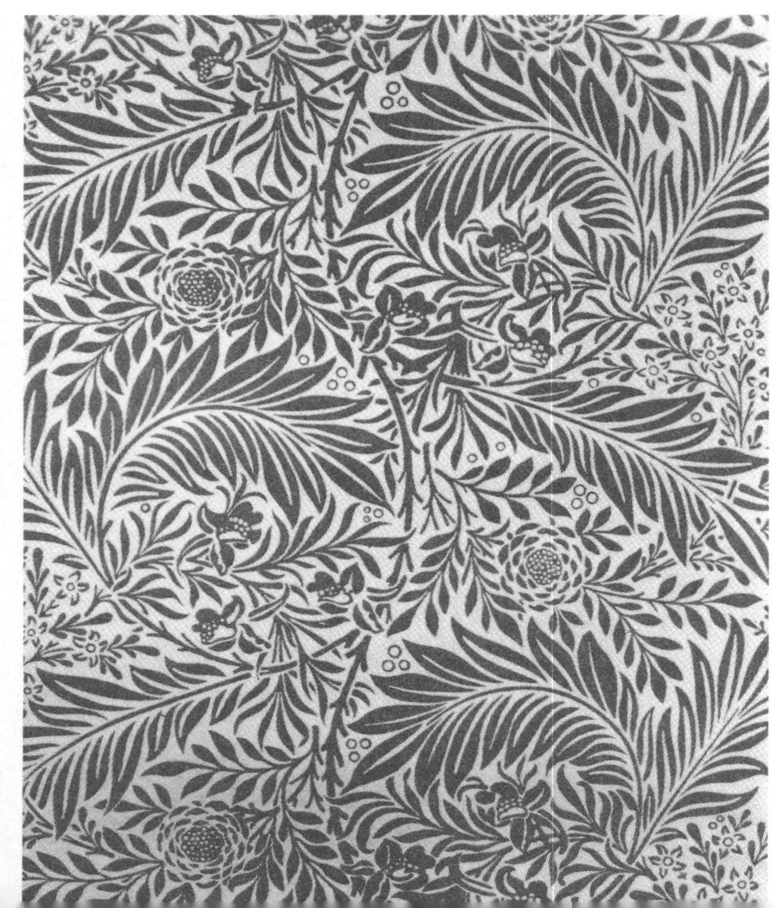

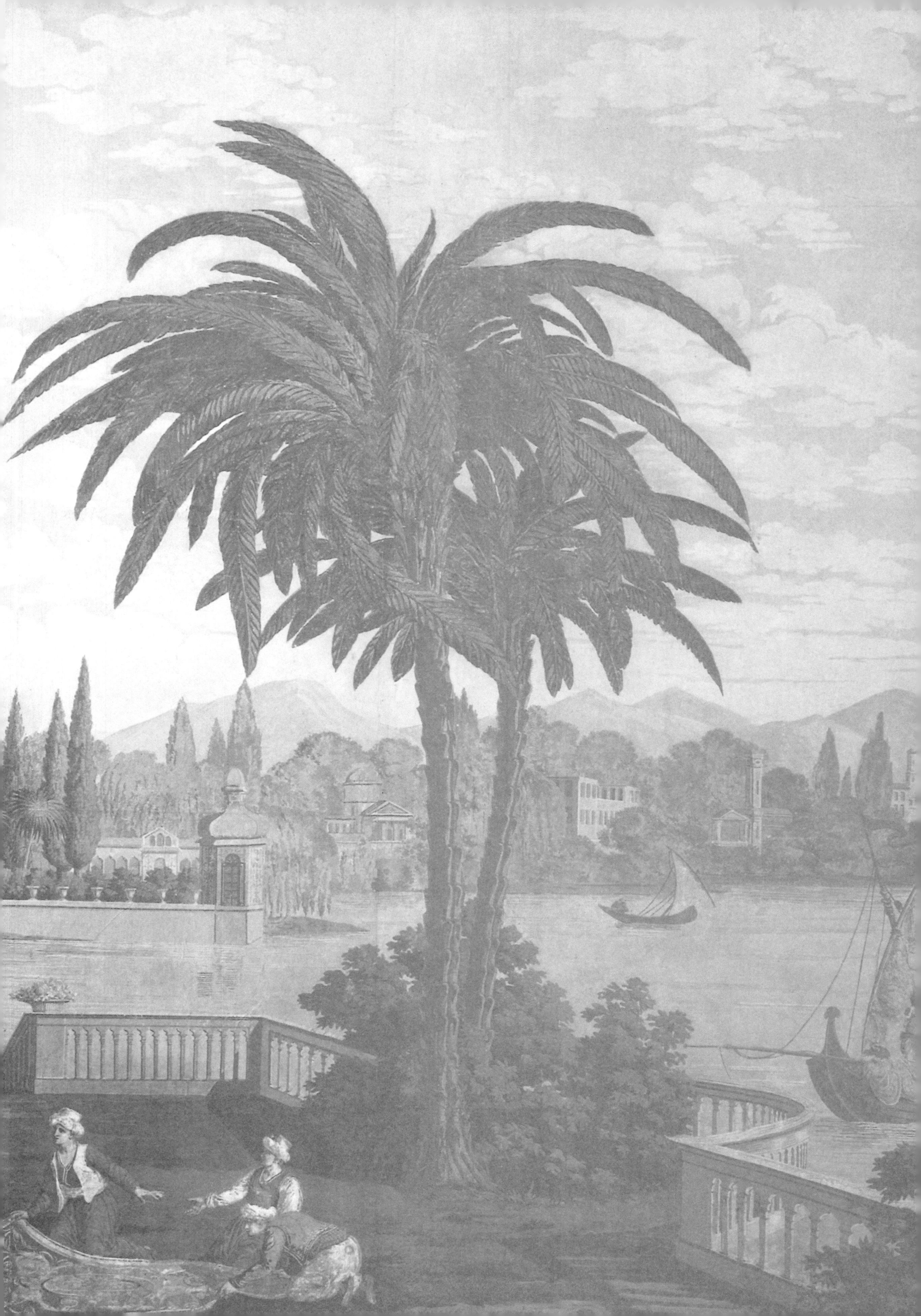

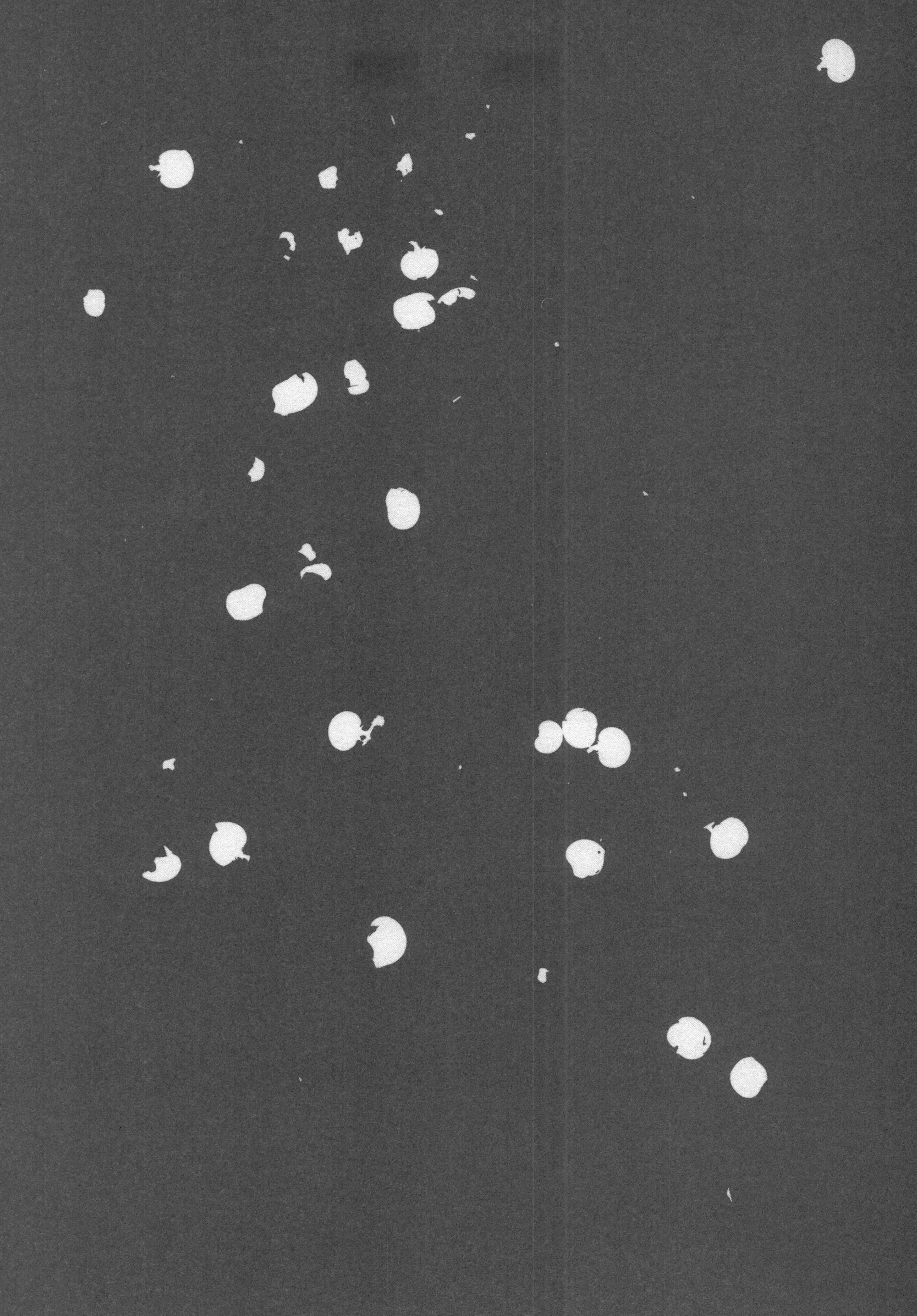

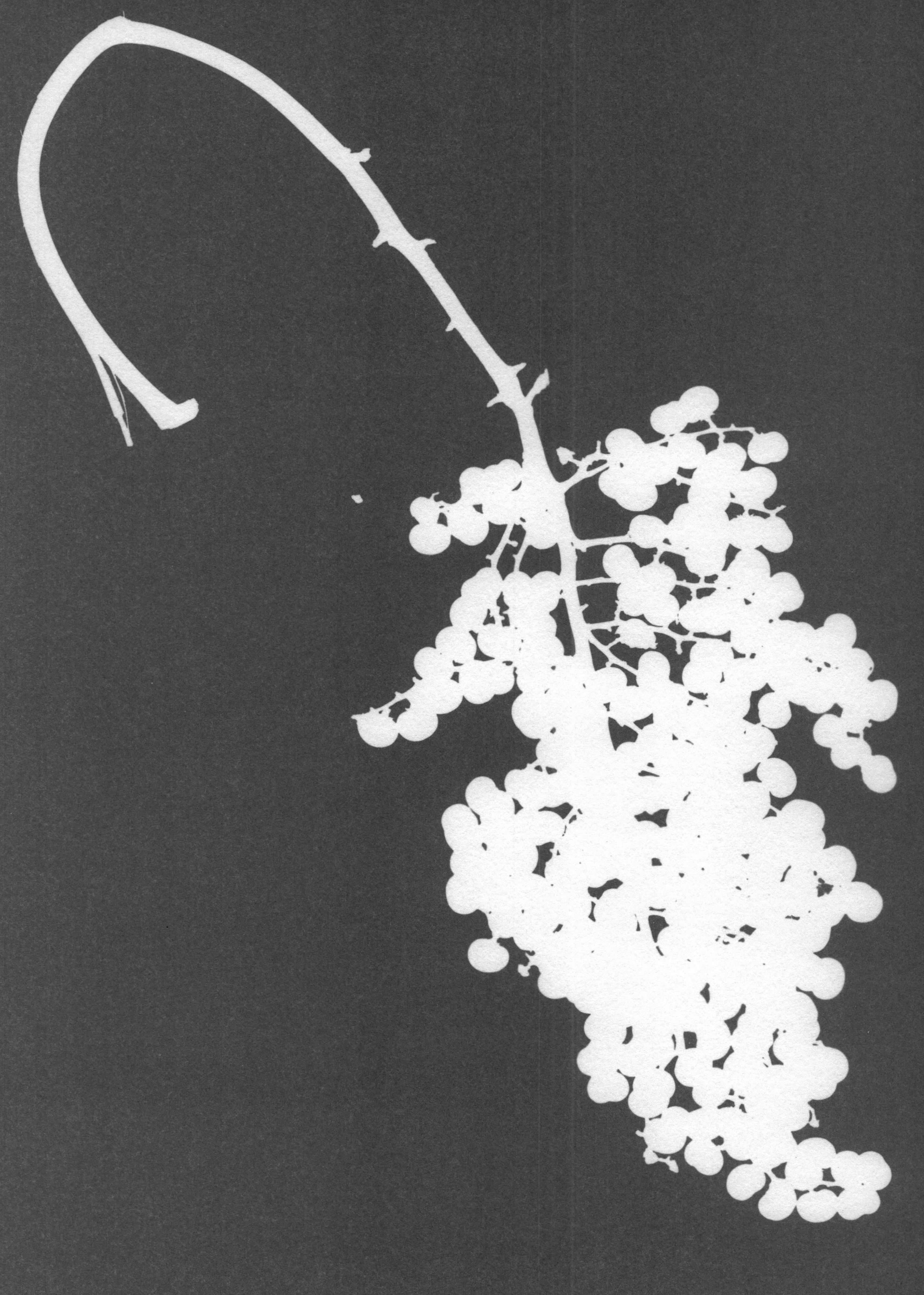

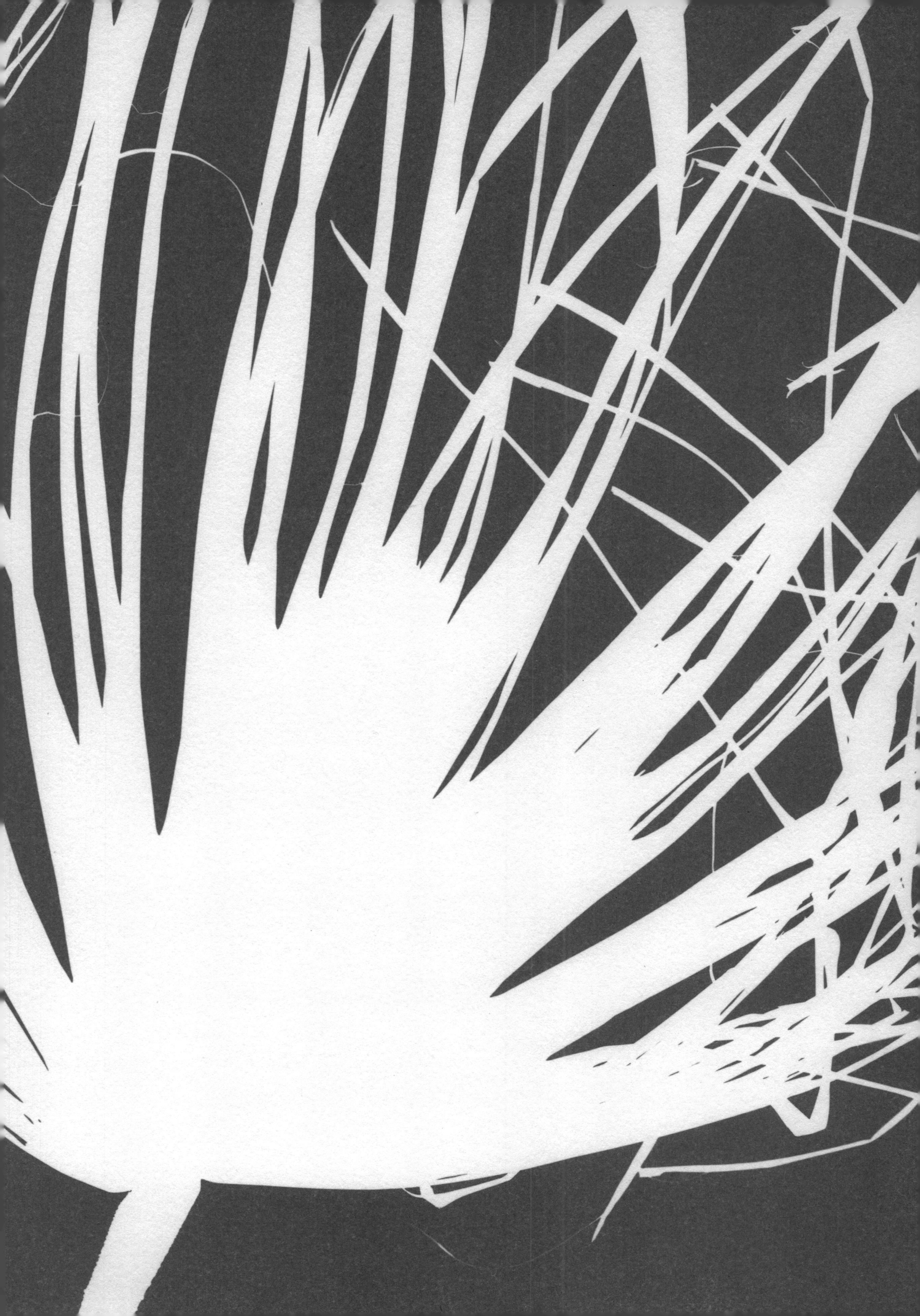

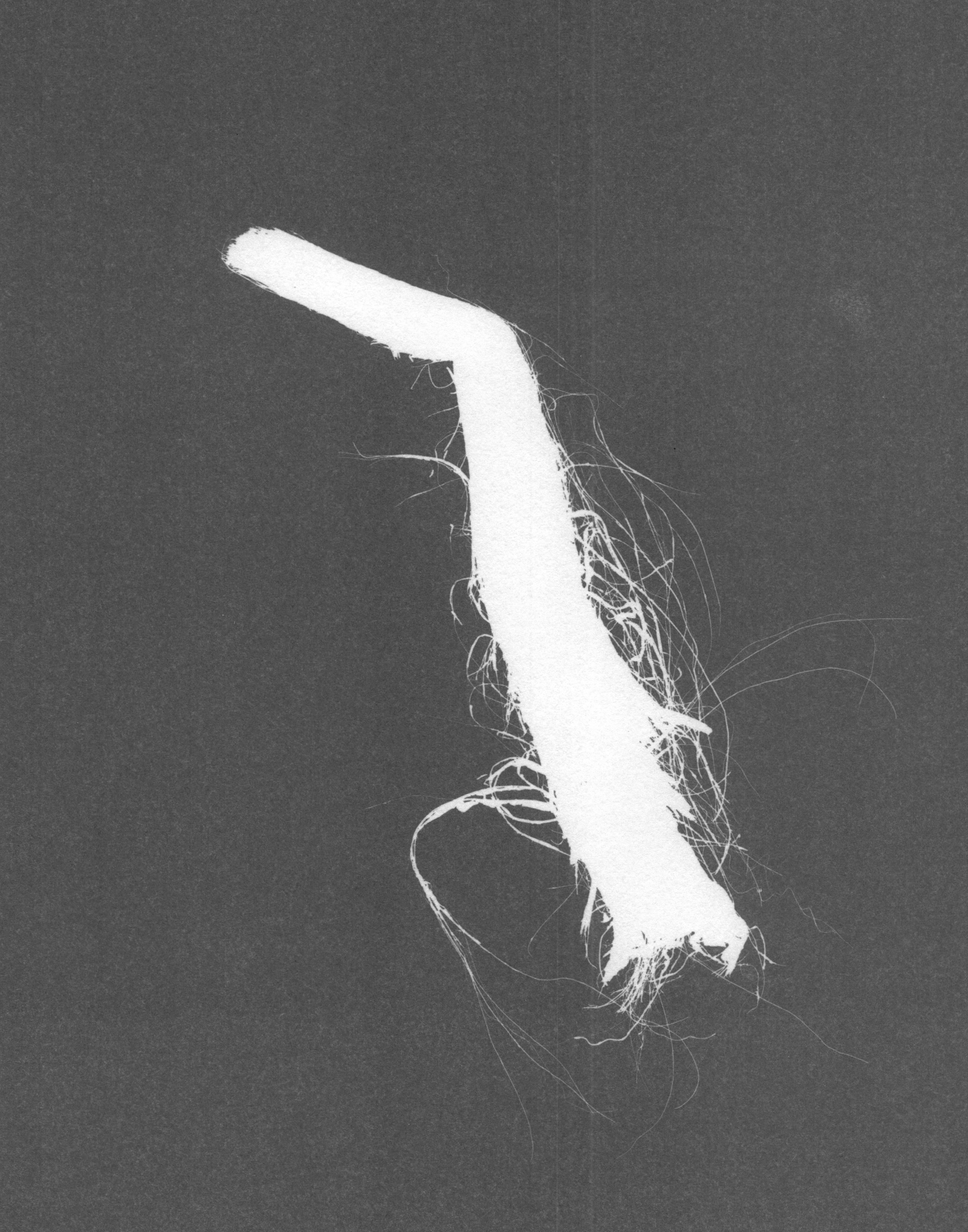

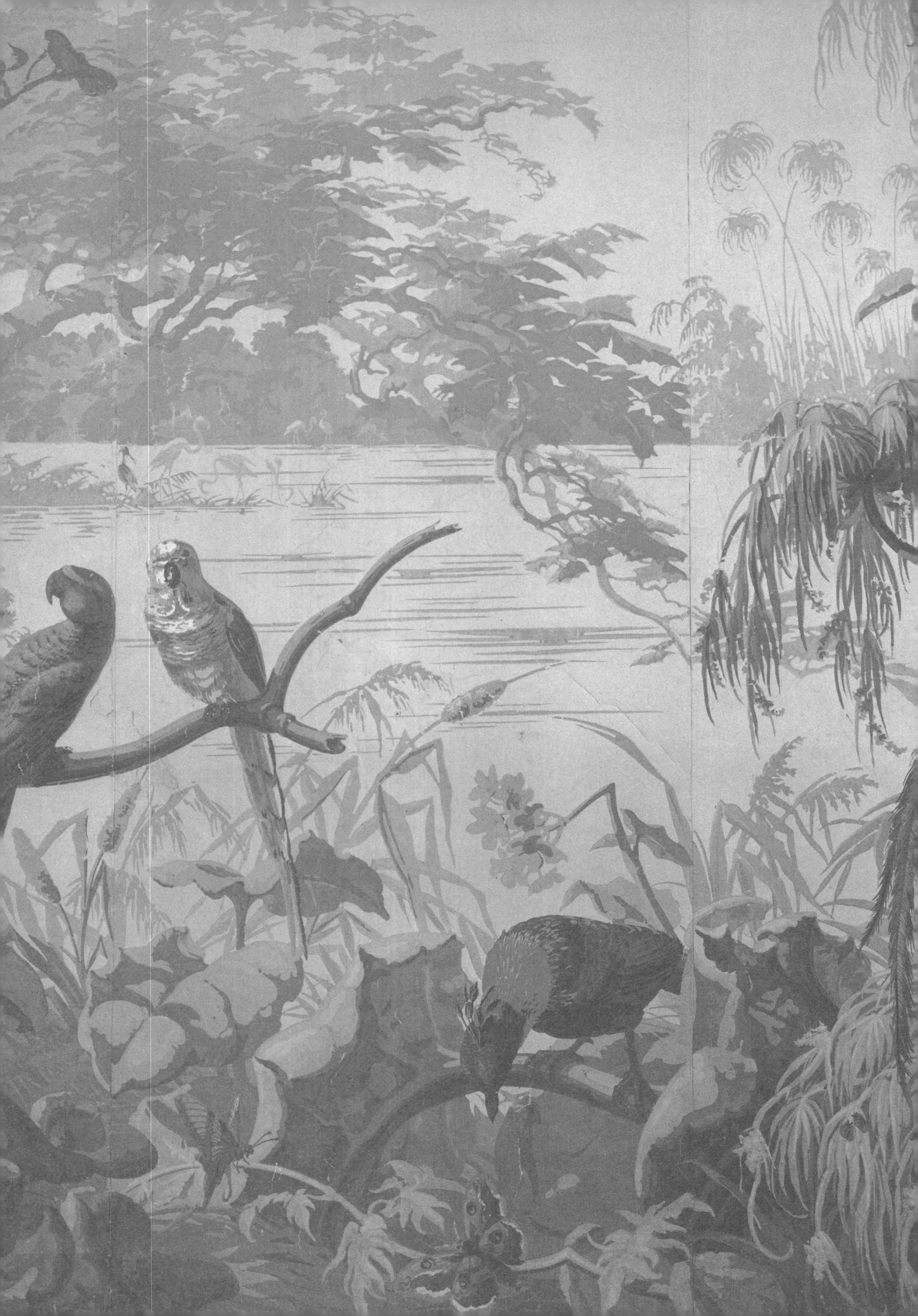

Palms as Décor

A conversation with Joanna Banham, Head of Public Programs at the Victoria & Albert Museum, London; curator of the exhibition *A Decorative Art: 19th Century Wallpapers*, Whitworth Art Gallery, Manchester (1985); and editor of Routledge's *Encyclopedia of Interior Design* (1997).

Nanna Debois Buhl: In the context of studying palm trees in South Tyrol, I am looking into how palms have been used in 19th-century décor. I know you have done extensive research on wallpapers and Victorian interiors. In this period, elements from the natural world of Asia appear in decorative arts as European craftspeople turned their gazes eastward. Can you give some examples of how they expressed their interest in an expanding world and its flora in wallpaper design?

Joanna Banham: You see depictions of nature on early 19th-century French panoramic wallpapers. The company Zuber et Cie created panoramas with titles such as *Views of Hindustan*, which were largely based on romantic views of India and South Asia. They depicted lots of palm trees and "exotic" landscapes. Another contemporary company, the Daniell Brothers, produced a series of books with colored lithographs entitled *Oriental Scenery*. They were used as sourcebooks for wallpaper manufacturers. Both cases express a taste for somewhere distant that looks rather mythologized. In the late 19th century, the designs by the Aesthetics Movement depicted a variety of Eastern elements and semi-exotic flora. Due to their strong interest in asymmetry and detail, those designs had a slightly more realistic quality than the more conventionalized flower and foliage depictions of the period just prior.

NDB: I have seen Chinoiserie—the use of Chinese visual elements in western design—described as a "wholly European style whose inspiration is entirely Oriental." The attempt was not to depict Chinese objects or landscapes as they were, but rather to create a visual imaginary of the "foreign" and "exotic." This method of blending of elements from various areas of the East seems to be shared by the very different craftspeople you just described.

JB: Yes, very much. China is a word that is used to cover most of the Far East. In general, there was very little distinction made between Japan, China, and other Far Eastern areas. The Chinese didn't actually use wallpapers themselves, so Chinese wallpapers were simply an export product for the European and North American markets. The wallpapers were inspired by Chinese painting of that time, which did not depict the world in a way that we would describe as realistic. The motifs were formalized scenes showing activities such as farming, growing rice, or making tea. In European decoration, these elements became even more stylized: a European imagination about this absolutely magical land of China, *Cathay.*

NDB: How do the varying visual treatments of plants and landscapes in the decorative arts of the 19th century relate to changing worldviews and views of nature?

JB: Any depiction of nature of that period should be considered alongside developments in science, the increasingly encyclopedic knowledge of the natural world, and the increasingly accurate ways people had of representing it. In painting, there was a connection between John Ruskin and the Pre-Raphaelites' very microscopic representation of nature and the discoveries by naturalists like Charles Darwin and others who were looking at the natural world and its geological strata. In the late 18th and early 19th century, there was also a large interest in mountains. People were attracted by mountain areas for their beautiful and sublime qualities. In the mid to late 19th century, there was a large interest in geological forms—in how the world was made, what it was made of, and how the laws of nature operate. I think those changing interests are mirrored in the decorative arts.

NDB: I wonder whether early botanical photography influenced wallpaper design. I am thinking of the photograms by Henry Fox Talbot and the cyanotypes by Anna Atkins. William Morris is a famous example of a designer working with floral motifs. What sources did he look at?

JB: For his wallpapers and textiles, William Morris used historical source books like John Gerard's 17th century book *The Herball*. The composition of the illustrations in herbals—which are early botanical reference books—are sort of unrealistic, because they attempt to show every possible view of a plant: an incredibly detailed drawing of a root is presented next to a leaf or a branch. In this time before photography, there was a need for accuracy because the herbals were used for scientific purposes. As far as I know, Morris didn't use photography as a source, but he used this earlier form of accurate botanical depiction.

NDB: I am particularly interested in palm trees as a motif in interior design. How are palm trees used as a motif in different ways in the 19th century?

JB: As mentioned, you see depictions of palm trees on the scenic wallpapers. In Owen Jones' seminal book, *The Grammar of Ornament* (1868), you find palm fragments such as leaves and trunks used in ornamental patterns. Palm motifs are widely used in late 19th-century buildings like railway stations, conservatories, and orangeries. That is because the shape of the palm tree, with its slender trunk and fan-shaped leaves, is particularly well suited to the iron constructions of the period. Some English hotels had palm courts, places where you would have tea or light refreshments. In those places, you would find decorations with palm tree motifs alongside actual palms. You see palms used in the décors of cruise liners. Palms appear in spaces for leisure where they are meant to suggest exotic travels, luxury, and warmth.

NDB: My project takes as its point of departure the northeastern Italian city Merano, where a large number of palm trees grow in parks and gardens. The first palms were brought there in the 1880s (from China via Britain) as the city was tranforming into a health resort and tourist destination. (How) could the Merano palm trees be read in a design historical framework?

JB: Again, I think it is a way of bringing in a bit of somewhere very far away and making an ordinary place seem more dramatic and unusual. Whoever planted the palms must have had quite a lot of horticultural advice in order to get the correct species for the area. The Merano palm trees are an interesting example of someone wanting to create a phantasmagorical space. But this fantasy could only be realized because of the increased knowledge about plants and nature and the progress in science and travel of the time.

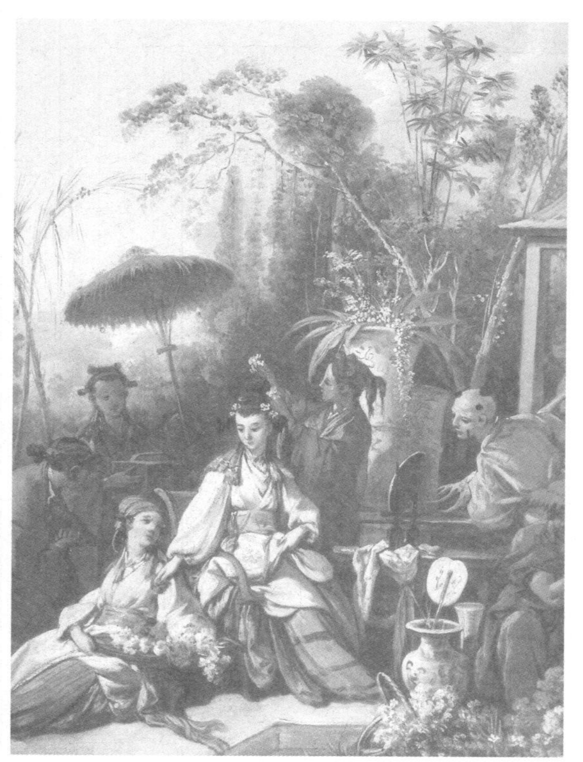
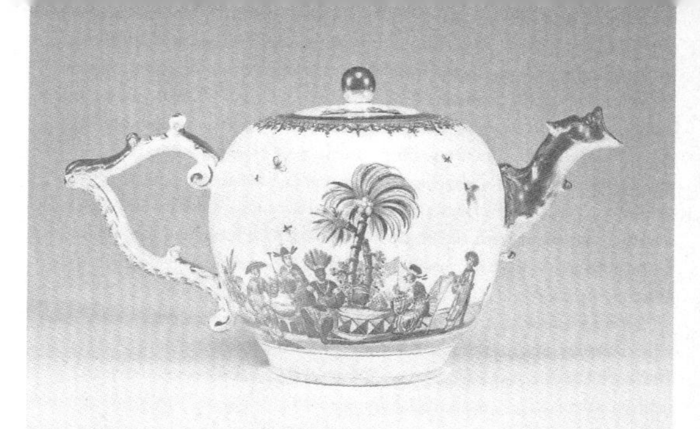

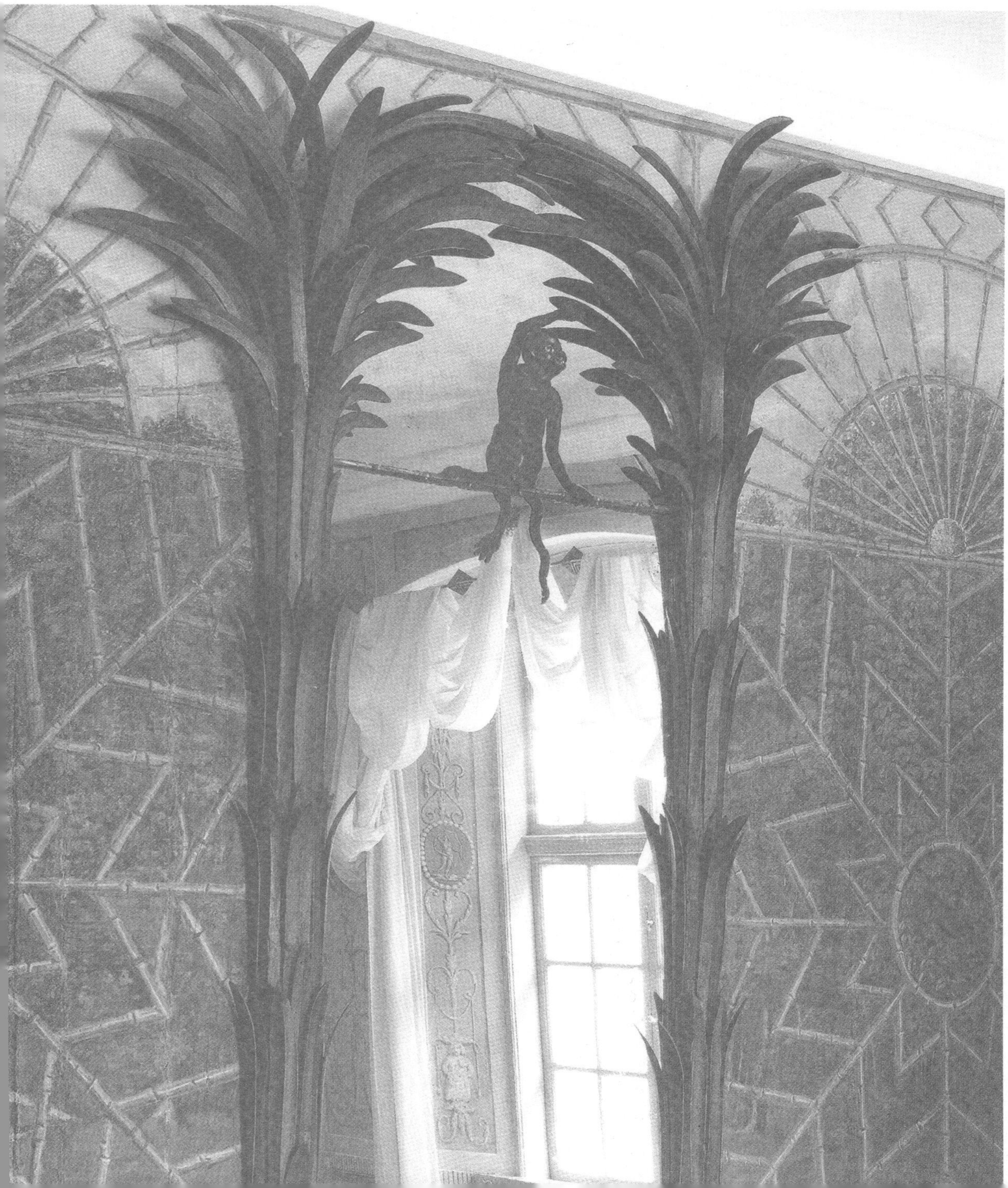

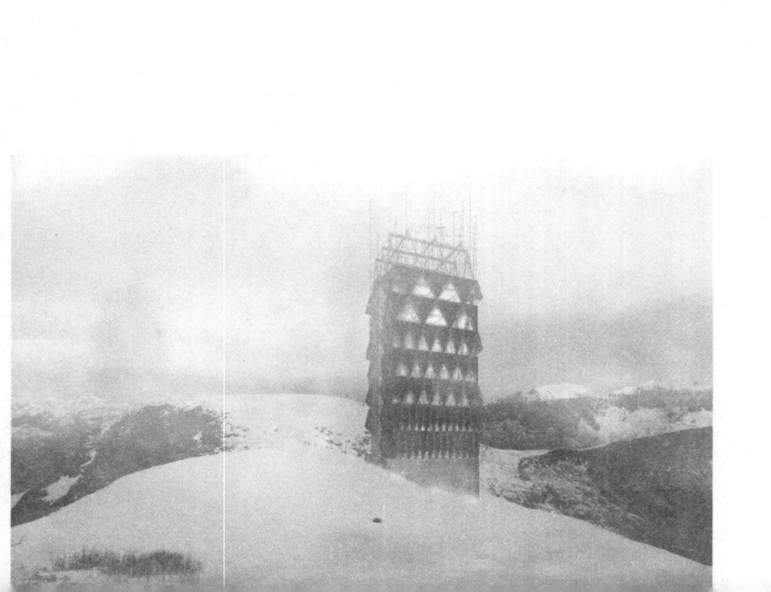

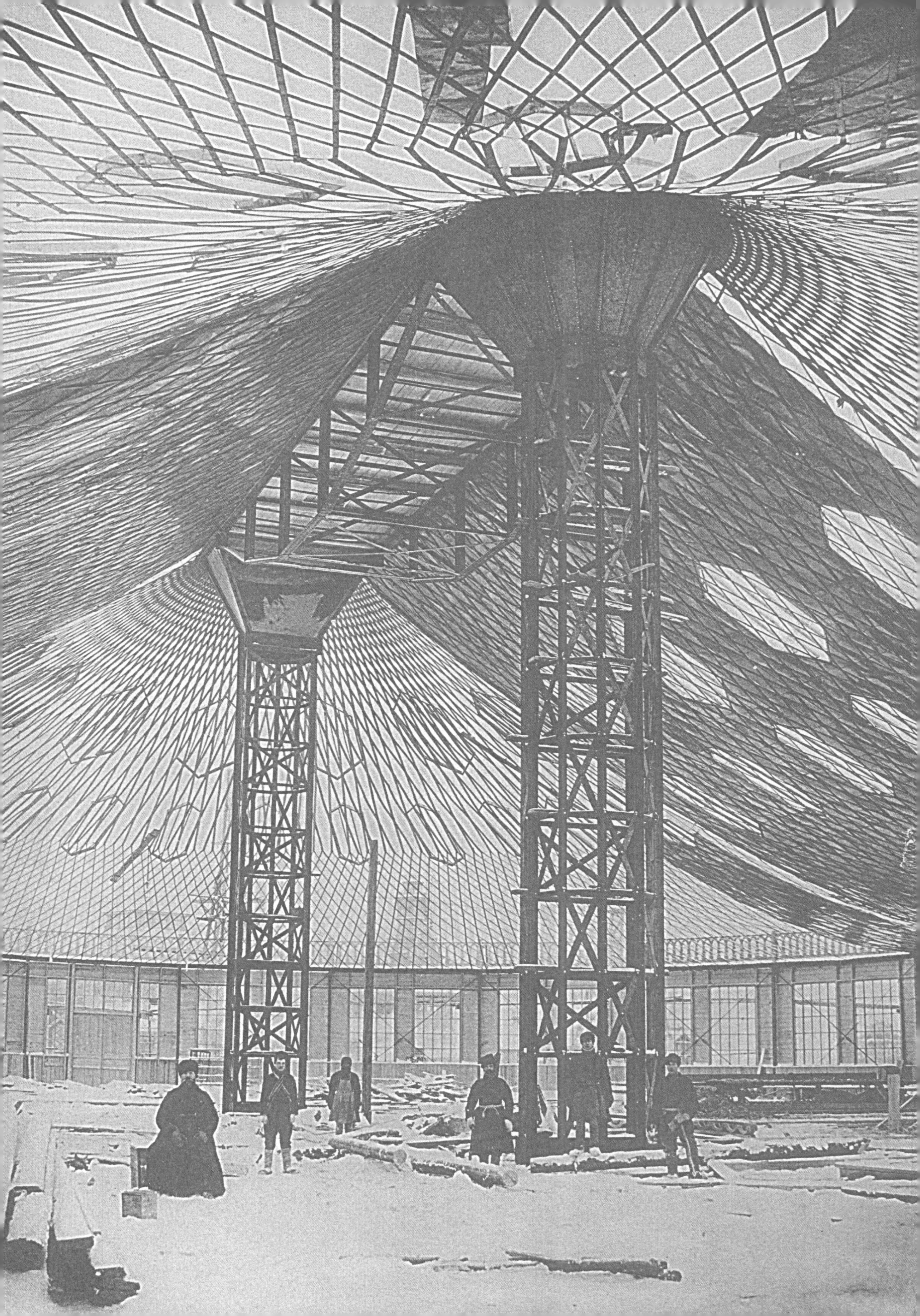

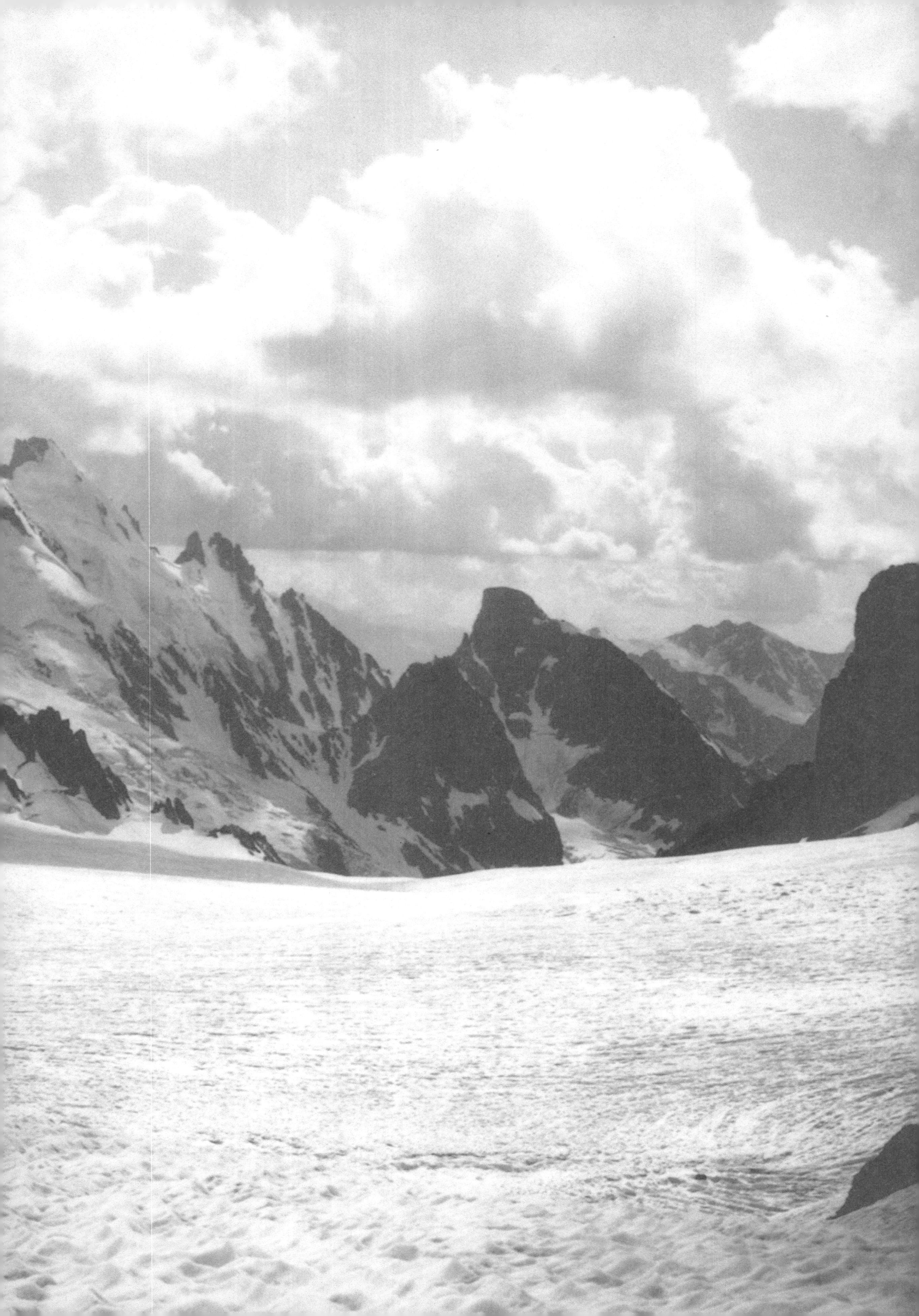

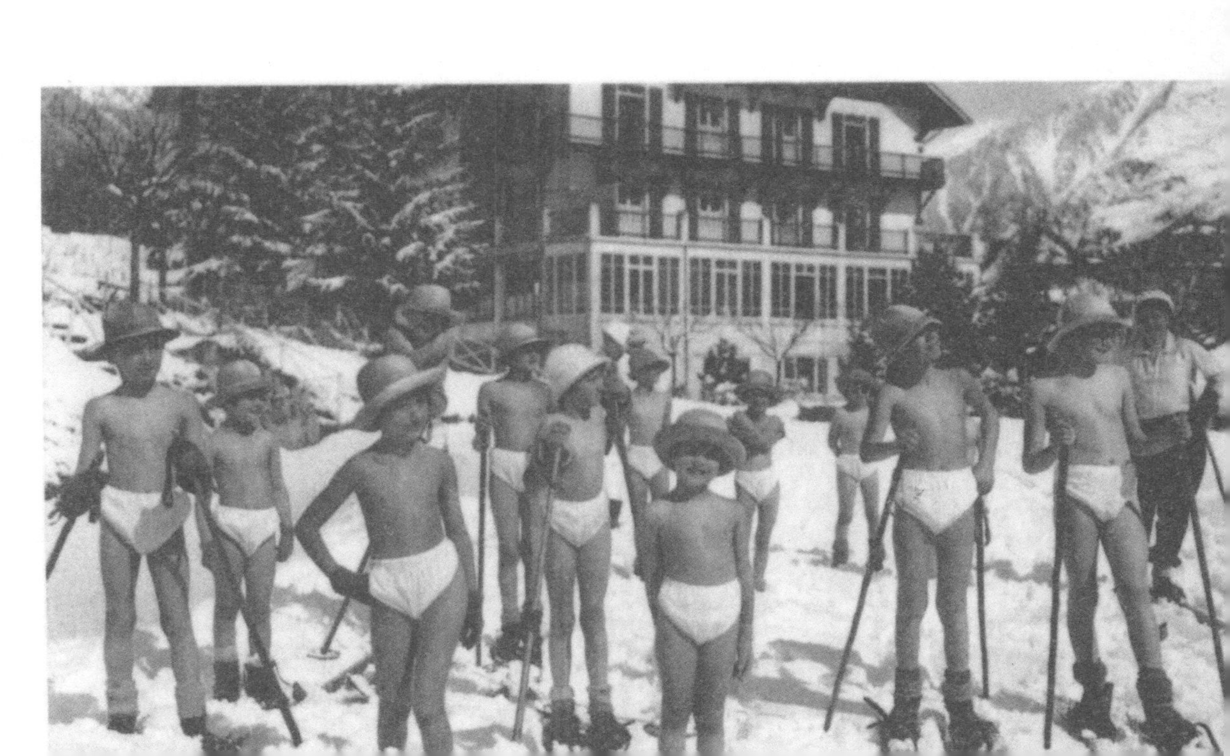

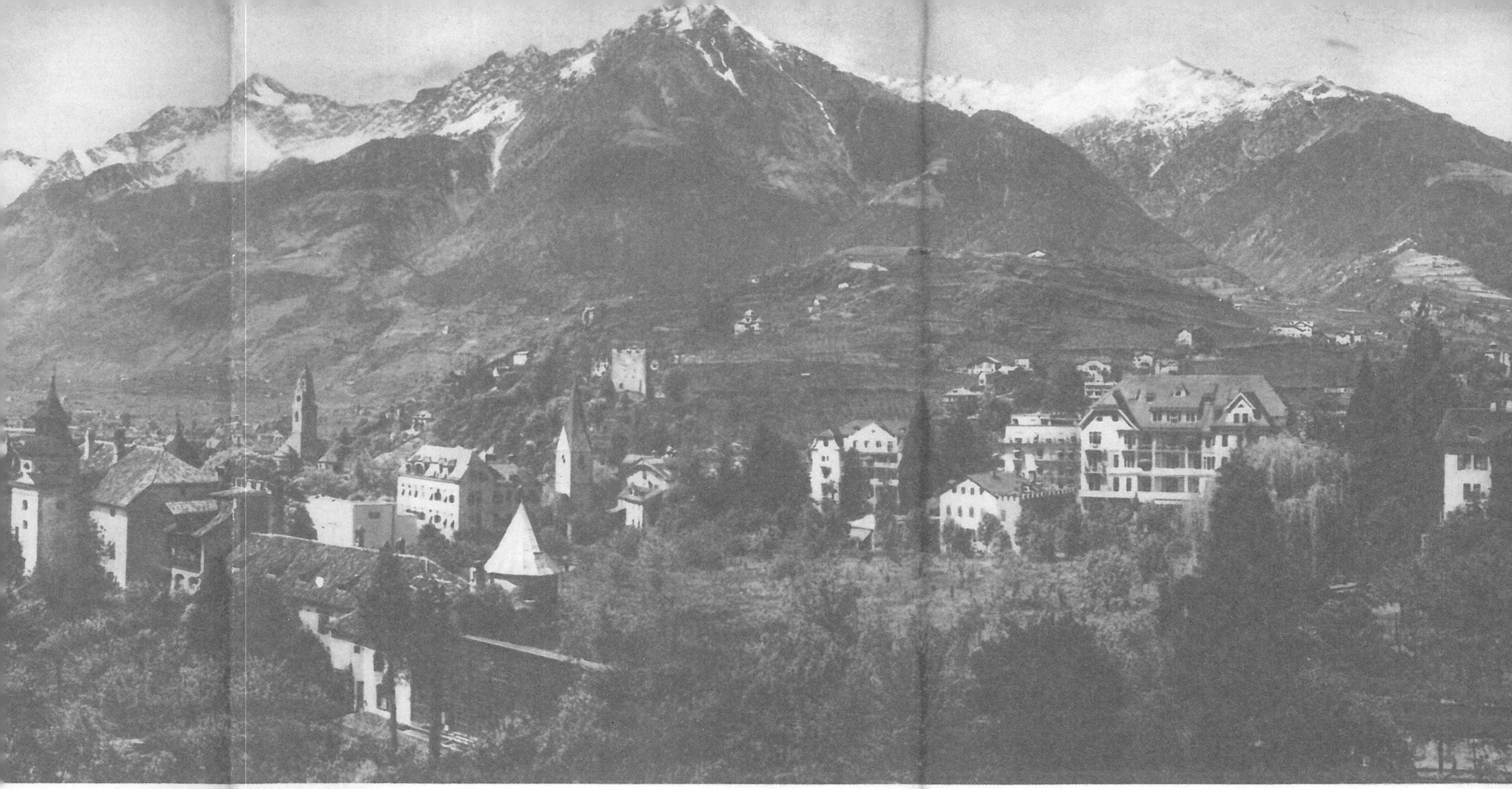

VEDUTA GENERALE   VUE GÉNÉRALE   GENERAL VIEW   GESAMTANSICHT

Alpine Dreams

A conversation with architect Susanne Stacher, curator of the exhibition *Dreamland Alps: Utopian Projections and Projects*, Kunst Meran (2014).

Nanna Debois Buhl: In the catalog to the *Dreamland Alps* exhibition, you describe how the Alps since the 18th century have been an ideal place for philosophical, utopian, and visionary reflections. What is it about the Alpine landscape that makes it such an attractive location for these reflections?

Susanne Stacher: For a long time, the Alps were the center of the sublime visions because they provoked very strong emotions between fear and ecstasy. Until the end of the 17th century, the dramatic Alpine landscape was associated with evil forces and the expulsion from Eden. In the early 18th century, utopian and political ideas of freedom began to be projected onto the Alps. Thomas More had already mapped his utopian ideas onto a fictitious island two hundred years earlier. By the end of the 18th century, British philosophers would project their utopian visions onto this existing geographical location of the Alps.

On their grand tours, the British aristocracy crossed the Alps on their way towards Rome. They passed through South Tyrol, the intermediate between the mountains and the cultivated landscape of Italy. Merano, which is situated here, offered a combination of dramatic mountain scenery associated with the sublime, and a mild climate that allowed for the existence of Mediterranean vegetation, even palm trees.

NDB: You bring up the notion of the *therapeutic landscape*, as several of the architectural projects in the *Dreamland Alps* exhibition are related to health and treatment. What role did Alpine nature play in 19th-century health resorts like Merano?

SS: By the time Merano is becoming a health tourism destination, it was (mistakenly) believed that the tuberculosis sanatoriums had to be placed at an altitude of at least 1500 meters in order to provide an efficient cure. Since the city was not situated high enough to be a suitable location for the tuberculosis treatments, it attracted a different clientele of people with less serious health conditions. In contrast to the sanatoriums, where the risk of contamination was high, Merano was a safe place to get a cure. Due to the many hours of sun in the Merano region, helio-therapeutic treatments were among the cures provided here.

NDB: So the landscape played a very crucial role, because there was a direct connection between factors like altitude and hours of sun, and the types of treatments the specific resorts could provide. What are the links—aesthetically and ideologically—between Alpine 19th-century health resorts and the sanatoriums of the 1920s?

SS: In 1882, the German physician Robert Koch discovered that tuberculosis was spread by bacteria. The architecture of the health resorts was impacted by this discovery, as from a medical point of view, ornamentation was to be avoided because ornate patterns were difficult to clean properly. However, it took several decades before the idea that ornament was a problem for hygiene began to have an impact. Of course this was linked to aesthetic discussions by architects like Adolf Loos who also argued against ornament—not for medical but for semantic reasons.

When the first tuberculosis sanatorium was founded by Dr. Karl Turban in Davos in 1889, it was built in the old style. It was only in the 1920s that sanatoriums became entirely devoid of ornamentation. Also, the removal of ornamentation had to be accepted by the patients and visitors. When the first sanatoriums without ornamentation were built, people didn't want to go there. They didn't want to be stigmatized as ill and outcasts by this modern architecture. They preferred the ornamental buildings because they looked like the Grand Hotels, which were not associated with disease.

NDB: You describe in the *Dreamland Alps*

catalog how the Alps were "discovered" by an urban civilization that started an ongoing "conquest" of nature in the 18th century. How have depictions of the Alps changed across time?

SS: In general, there was as shift in the depiction of mountain areas. The romantic paintings of the mountains in the early 19th century were linked to the ideas of the sublime. By the late 19th century, artificial mountain landscapes would be popular attractions in world fairs. In amusement parks, you would find mountain-themed roller coasters, as well as diorama shows that also depicted mountains.

When people who had seen these representations went to visit the real Alps, they were disappointed because the mountain landscape did not live up to their expectations. Therefore, there was an attempt to make the mountain regions more attractive by illuminating waterfalls or by decorating the Grand Hotels with antlers and stuffed bears. Many things were done in order to make the mountains seem even more sublime than they actually were. Maybe the Merano palm trees could also be seen in this context. They are one of those extra elements added to a landscape in order to fulfill the expectations for spectacle.

NDB: It seems like there is a sense of longing toward an imaginary elsewhere in many of the projects presented in the *Dreamland Alps* exhibition. I have also seen Merano described as "The Italian Shangri-La." Is this longing a recurring phenomenon related to the Alps?

SS: Yes, very much. I think this longing for a "somewhere else" is also central for the period: a longing for a place different from the mundane world and an attraction towards wild nature, mountains, and islands. Those places were then carefully constructed. Merano is an example of this with its blend of many elements: panoramic mountains, Mediterranean climate, health resort culture and, with the palm trees, a fantasy of the East.

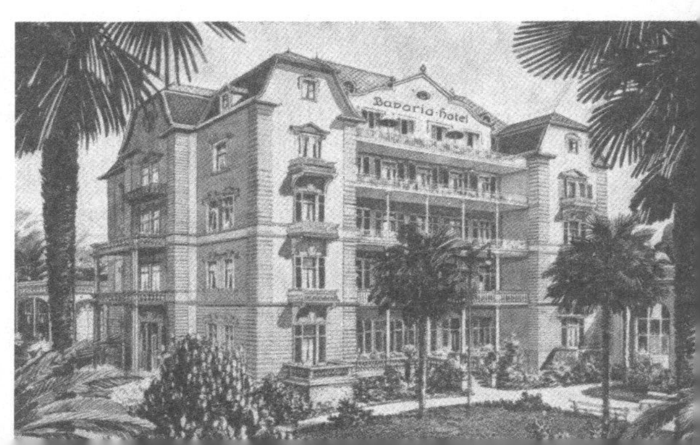

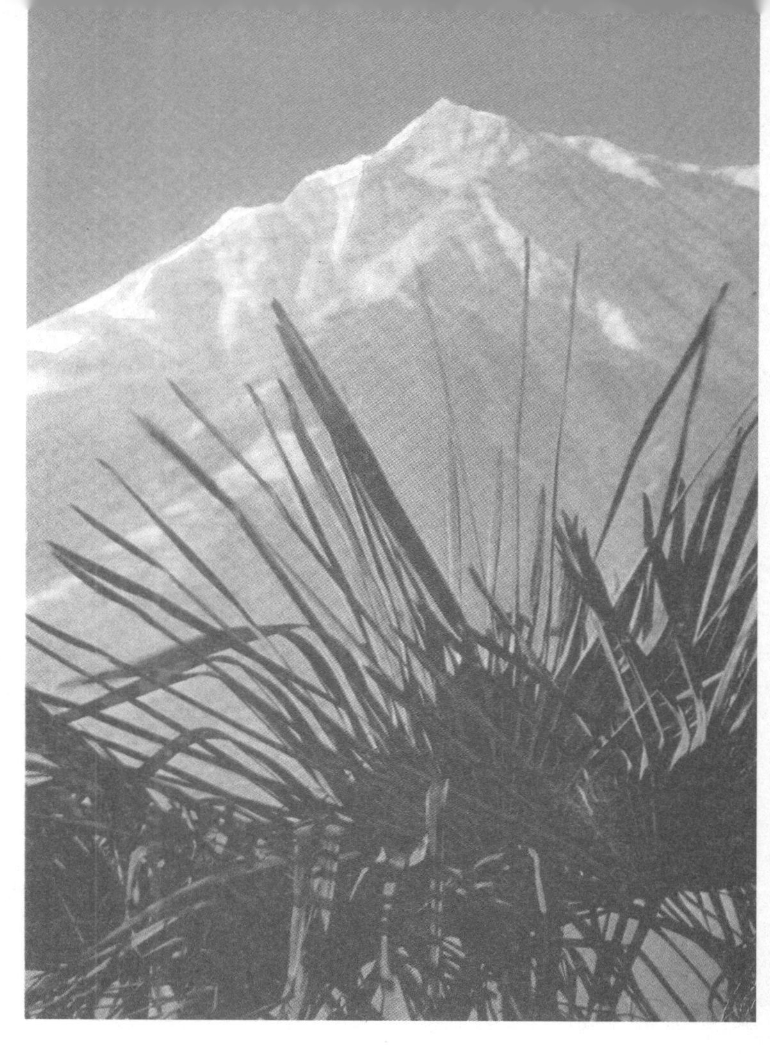

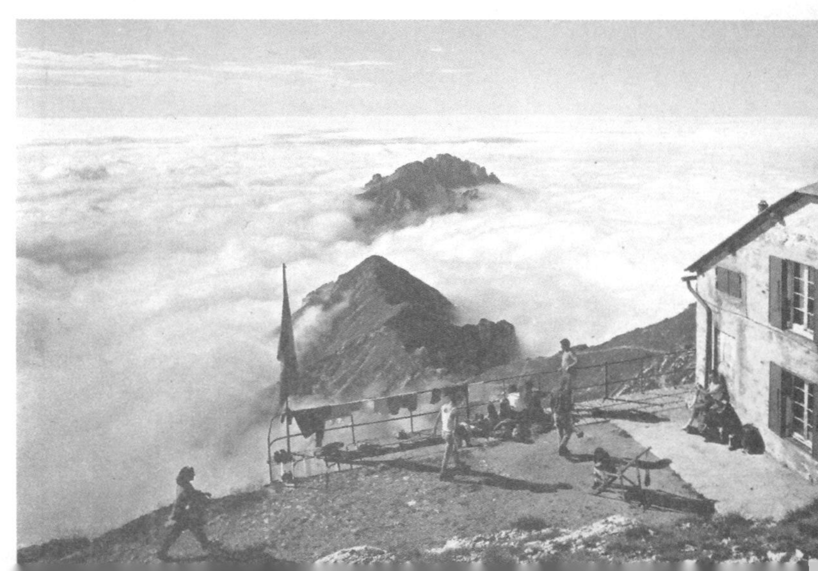

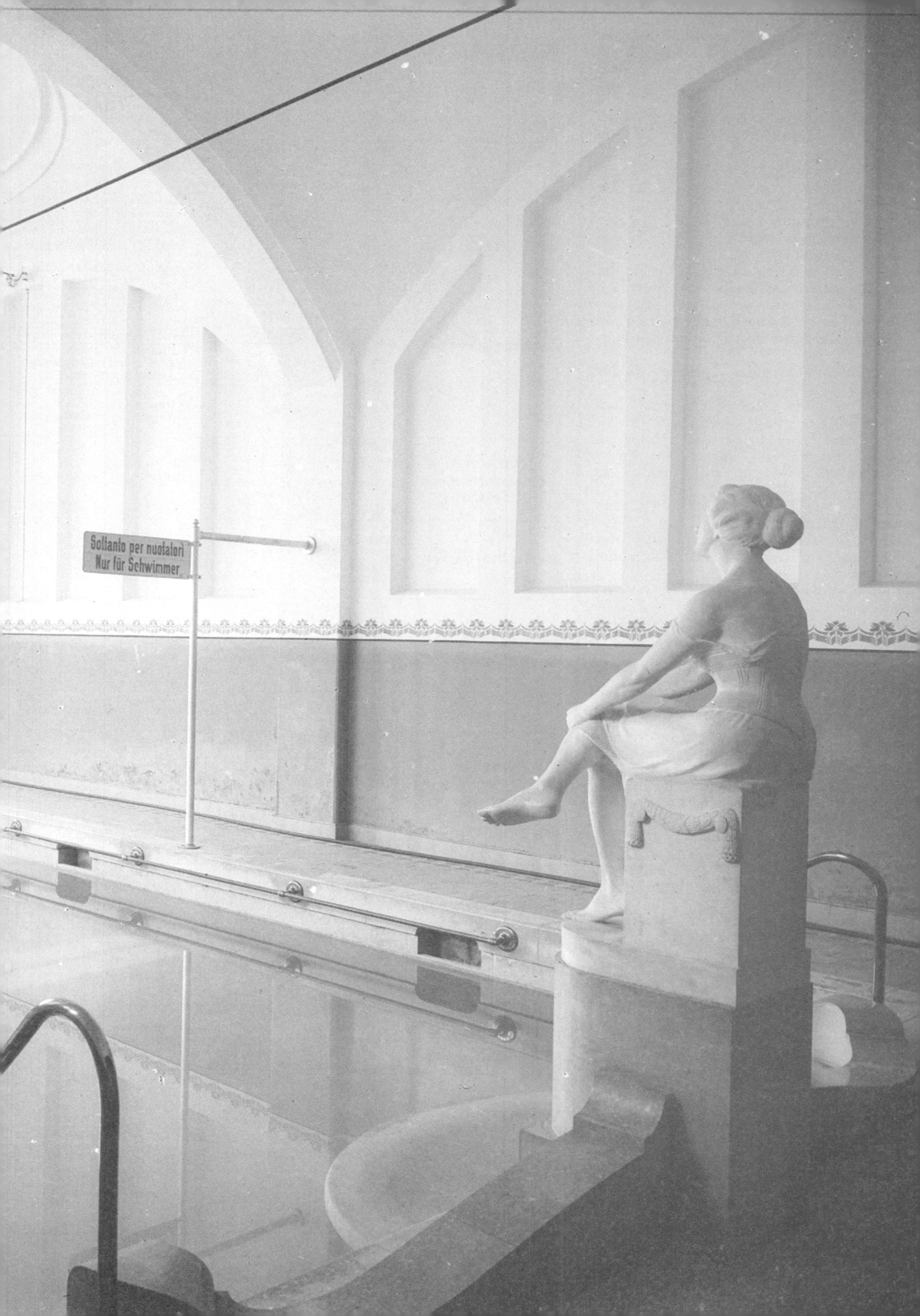

Soltanto per nuotatori
Nur für Schwimmer

en Kurgästen gegenüber bei Benützung
tze um die gebotene Zurückhaltung ge-
rsonen, welche durch Kleidung
ragen Anstoß erregen, sind
nslos durch die Aufsichtsorgane ab-

irbeln von Staub durch nicht fuß-
eider der Damen ist strengstens

age auf den Promenaden und ins-
in der Nähe des Musikpavillons ist
ichkeit freizuhalten.
n und Herumlaufen der Kinder in der
Musikpavillons während der Prome-
erte ist untersagt.
chen ist untersagt: a) vor dem
mit Ausnahme des Teiles der Terrasse
Restauration und längs der Passer;
Wandelbahnen der Kuranlagen; c) in
Anlagen während der Promenadenkon-

ind in sämtlichen Anlagen an der
ühren.
(mit Ausnahme der Rollwägen) und
st in allen Kuranlagen verboten.
eißen von Pflanzen und Blumen
stens untersagt und haben die Park-
ie Dawiderhandelnden zur Anzeige zu

en der Plätze (Stühle, Bänke) während
stunden ist nicht gestattet.
Wandelhallen ist das Stehenlassen der
en sowie den Kindern das Spielen und
ntersagt.
elhallen dürfen mit Rollwägen nicht
werden.
rsucht, zum Ausspucken die Spucknäpfe
en.

nung für das Kurhaus Meran.

aus ist im Frühjahr und Herbst von 7
bis 10 Uhr abends, im Winter von 8 Uhr
Uhr abends geöffnet.
(ohne Ausnahme), welche durch Klei-
Betragen Anstoß erregen, können aus
itäten entfernt werden.
t gestattet, in die Lokalitäten des Kur-
nde mitzunehmen.
hen (mit Ausnahme bei Unterhaltungen
derer Anzeige hiefür) ist nur in der
on und im Café gestattet.
haltungen usw. wird nur für die in der
hinterlegten Kleider gehaftet.
genschirme sind dem Diener zur Aufbe-
u übergeben.
einzelne Lokalitäten behufs Vorberei-
Unterhaltungen oder infolge Komitee-
zeitweise geschlossen, so wird dies
schlag bekannt gegeben.
ersagt, Fenster, welche mit der Inschrift
tung" geöffnet sind, eigenmächtig zu

h alle nur erdenklichen Maßregeln gegen
ahr im Hause angewendet sind, so wird
nerksam gemacht, daß bei allen Unter-
sämtliche Türen, gegen die Promenade
die Haupttreppe zu, immer offen sind.
re Verweilen in den Korridoren des Kur-
wie die Benützung der dort befindlichen
nd Fauteuils zum Liegen ist nicht ge-

Kurhaus Besuchenden haben die Haus-
zu beobachten und den Weisungen des
ersonals Folge zu leisten. Allenfallsige
den sind in der Kurkanzlei anzubringen.

Wasserheilverfahren (Hydrotherapie)	Halbbäder, Sitz- und Fussbäder (auch fliessend), Einpackungen, Wassertreten, Lakenabreibung, Teilfrottierung, Umschläge, Kühlapparate, temperierte Douchen, Blitzdouchen, Güsse, Dampfdouchen	Kurmittelhaus der Stadt (Direktor Dr. Schmidt) Dr. Ballmann's Wasserheilans[talt] Hotel Maendlhof Dr. Binder's Sanatorium St San.-Rat Dr. von Kaan's [Sana]torium Martinsbrunn, Gra[z] Wassermann's Kurabteilung [h] in der Kurpension Eden Dr. Rodlers Kurabteilung Pension Aders
Thermotherapie	Elektr. Lichtbäder für den ganzen Körper u. einzelne Teile, Schlammpackungen (Fango, Schwefelschlamm) und Lichtbestrahlungen	Alle Anstalten wie oben
	Heissluftbäder und Douchen	Alle Anstalten wie oben und [ortho]pädisches Institut Villa L[ourdes]
	Thermopenetration (Transthermie)	Sanatorium Martinsbrunn Sanatorium Stefanie
Elektrotherapie	Elektrische, galvanische, faradische, Wechselstrom-, Voll- und Vierzellenbäder	Alle Anstalten wie oben
	Galvanisation, Faradisation, Voltaisation	Alle Anstalten wie oben, dem orthopädisches Institu[t] die meisten Kurärzte
	Franklinisation	Alle Anstalten wie oben
	d'Arsonval	Maendlhof, Obermais Sanatorium Martinsbrunn Sanatorium Stefanie
	Röntgen	Maendlhof, Obermais Meraner Heilanstalt Sanatorium Martinsbrunn Sanatorium Stefanie
Radium-Emanationsbehandlung	Radium-Emanations-Inhalatorium (Emanatorium) von hoher Intensität. Radioaktive Bäder aus Joachimstaler Pechblende. Emanations-Trinkkuren	Kurmittelhaus Sanatorium Stefanie
	Radioaktive Bäder mit Zusätzen	Alle Anstalten wie oben
Medizinalbäder	Kohlensaure Bäder (aus flüssiger Kohlensäure), kohlensaureSolbäder, Sol-, Steinsalz-, Meersalz-, Fichten-, Kräuter-, Kiefermoor-, Moorsalz-, Moorlaugen-, Jod-, Schwefel- und Sauerstoff-Bäder	Alle Anstalten wie oben
	medico-mechanisches Zander-Institut	Kurmittelhaus Sanatorium Stefanie
Mechanotherapie	Heilgymnastische Apparate, hygienisches Turnen, schwedische Heilgymnastik, Ataxie-Behandlung	Kurmittelhaus Orthopädisches Institut Villa L[ourdes] Sanatorium Stefanie Sanatorium Martinsbrunn Kurabteilung Hygiea, Eden
Orthopädie	Orthopädische Verbände, orthopädische Spezialbehandlung	Orthopädisches Institut, Jungwirth und Dr. v. Villa Lourdes
Massage	Hand-, elektrische u. Vibrationsmassage	Alle Anstalten wie oben, au[ch] die meisten Kurärzte
	Schwedische Massage	Kurmittelhaus Sanatorium Stefanie Orthopäd. Institut Villa Lo[urdes]
Inhalations- und pneumatische Therapie	Rauminhalation Systeme Clar und Bulling, einzeln und gemeinsam, lokale Inhalation (Hoesle u. Bulling) Pneumatische Kammer (8 Pers.) pneumat. Apparate Dupont-Matthieu	Kurmittelhaus
Dampf-, Schwimm- und Wannenbäder		Kurmittelhaus
Sonnen- und Luftbad		Kurmittelhaus Sanatorium Stefanie Sanatorium Martinsbrunn
Mineralwasserkuren, Traubensaft		Trinkhalle in der Wandelh[alle]
Laktotherapie	Yoghurt, Kefir, Molke, Trockenfuttermilch, kontrollierte Milch saure Milch, Rahm	Trinkhalle in der Wandelh[alle] Lasnauski, Milchtrinkhalle, Plankenstein Alle Apotheken und Sana[torien]
Terrainkuren	Eine reiche Auswahl von Promenaden u. Gehwegen (zum Teil von weil. Prof. Oertel persönlich markiert), in der Ebene, sanft ansteigend, oder mäßig steil, ermöglichen die Durchführung der Terrainkuren	In allen Kurgemeinden Untermais, Obermais und [Gratsch] des Kurortes und in der n[ächsten] Umgebung
Diätkuren	Für Zucker-, Nieren-, und sonstige Stoffwechselkranke, bei Unterernährung, Fettsucht und Blutarmut, für innere und Nervenkranke	In strenger Weise in 3 dia[tetisch] physikalischen Sanatorien, dem in zahlreichen Hote[ls] Pensionen
Sanatorien für physikalisch-diätetische Therapie	Für innere, Herz-, Nerven- und Stoffwechselkranke	Sanitätsrat Dr. v. Kaan's [Sana]torium, Martinsbrunn - G[raz] Dr. Binder's Sanatorium Kuranstalt Waldpark
Sanatorium für Lungenkranke	Spezialistische Anstaltsbehandlung von Erkrankungen der Atmungsorgane	Villa Hungaria, Untermais
Städtische Heilanstalt (Krankenhaus)	Interne Abteilung (Direktor Dr. Frank) Chirurgische Abteilg. mit großen aseptischen Operations-Sälen (Primarius Dr. Hofmann) Chirurgisches Ambulatorium	Forsterstrasse

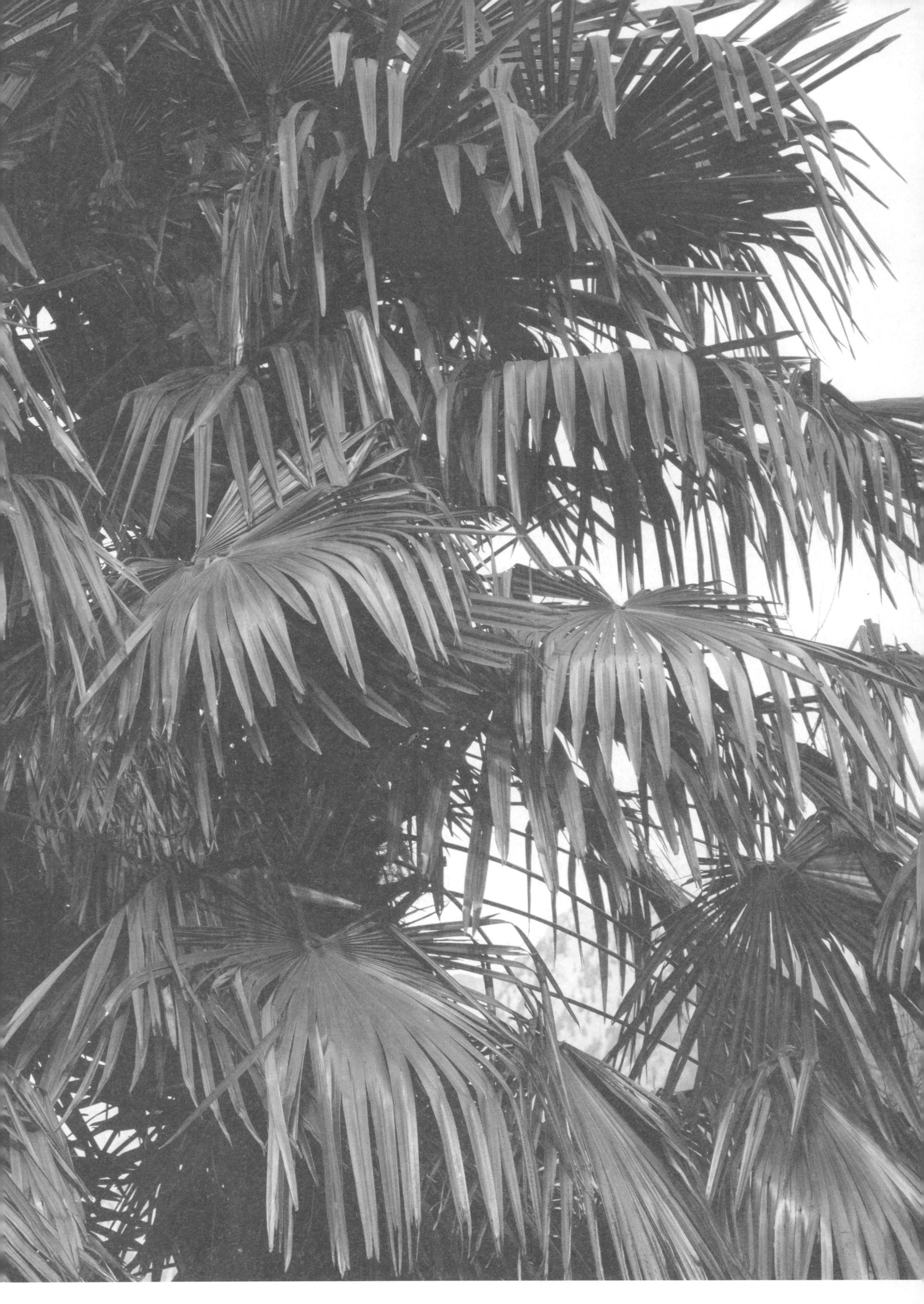

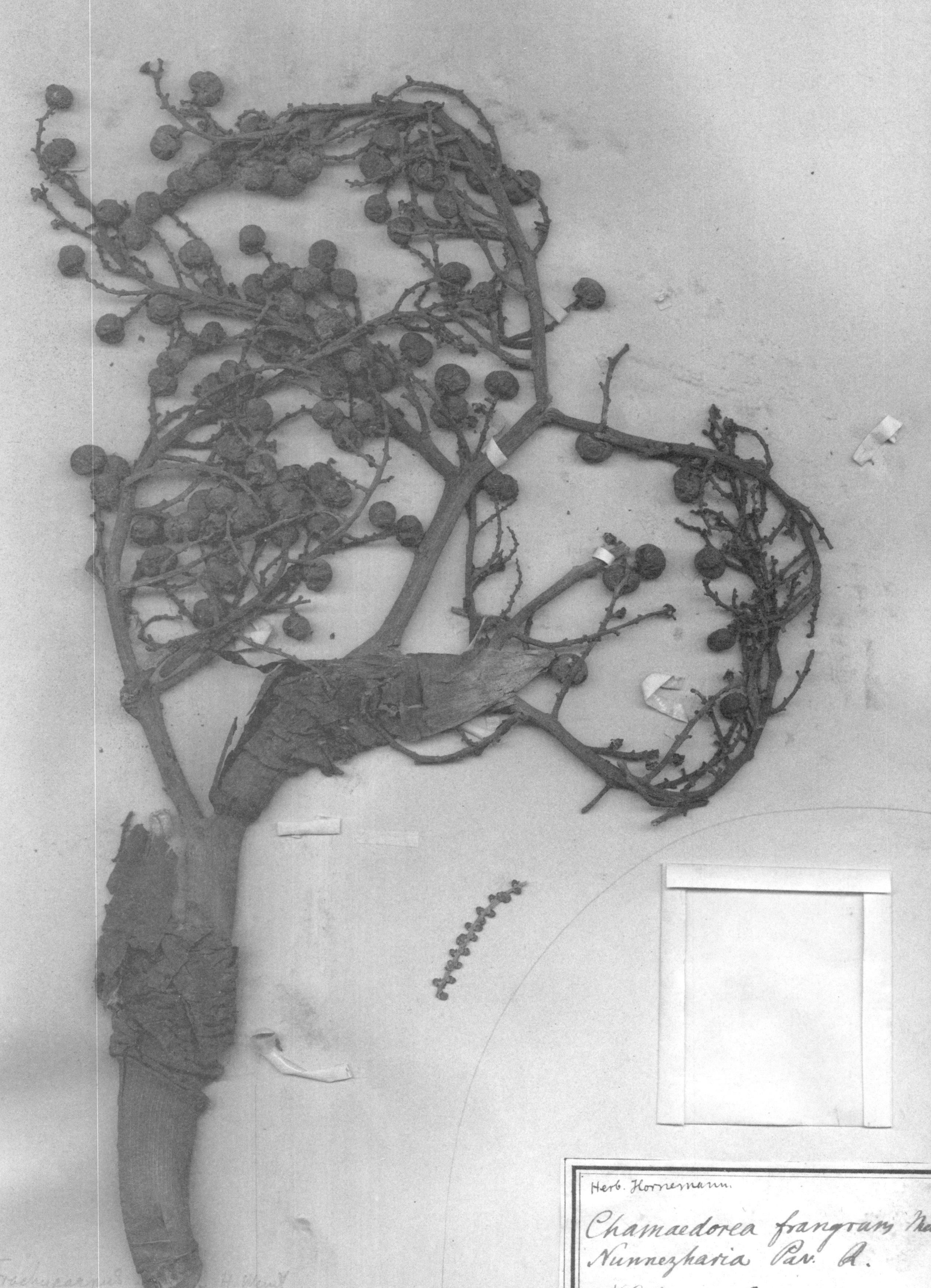

Trachycarpus ... H. Wendl.
(scripsit O. Beccari).
Herb. Hornemann.
Chamaedorea fragrans Ma...
Nunnezharia Pav. ...
Habitat in Peruvia

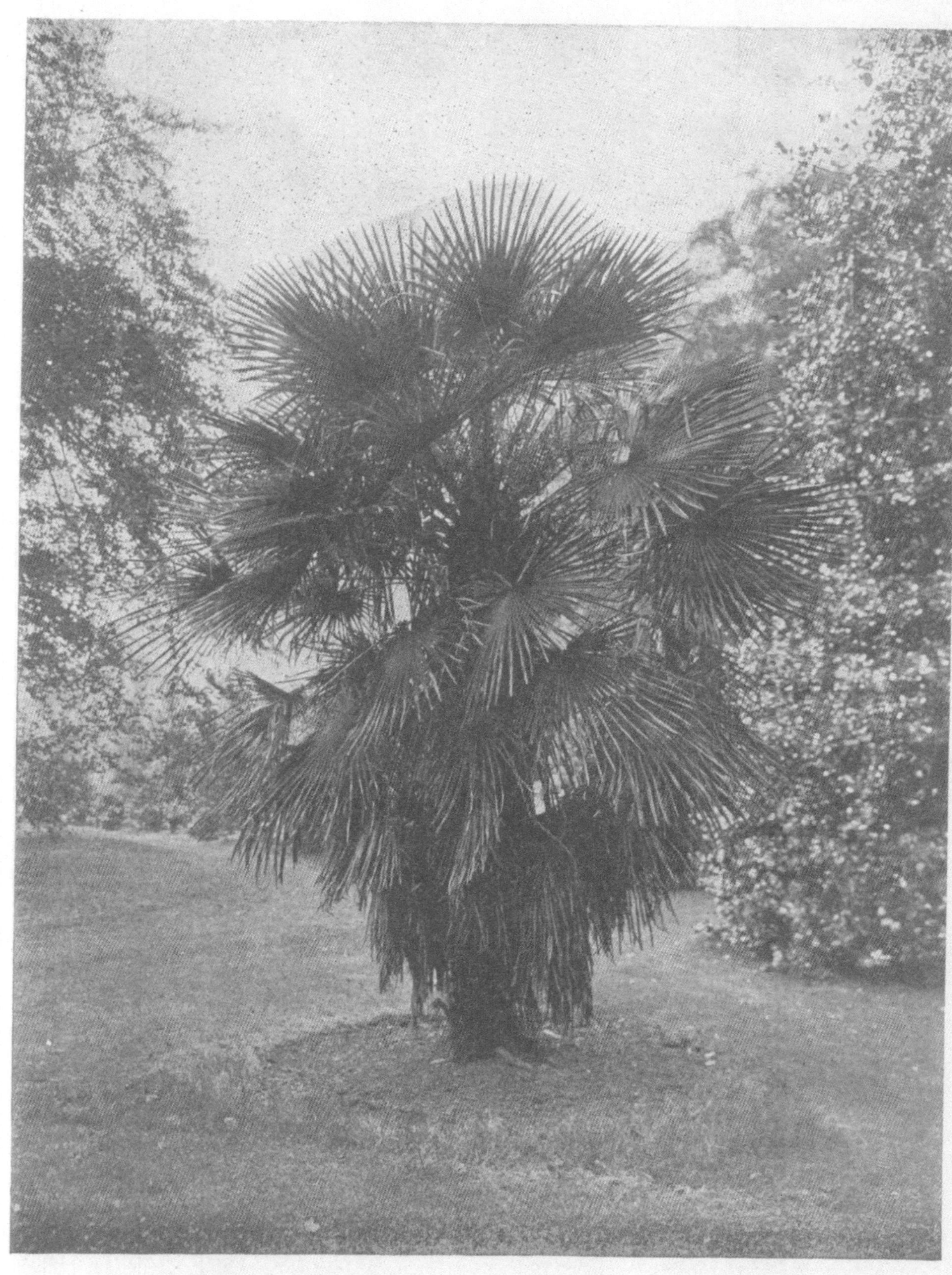

PLATE 33.—TRACHYCARPUS FORTUNEI, Chusan Palm

Sources

Enrico Banfi and Gabriele Galasso, *Diffusione e invasività della palma Trachycarpus fortunei,* Memorie della Società Italiana di Scienze Naturali e del Museo Civico di Storia Naturale di Milano, 2008

Joanna Banham (ed.), *Encyclopedia of Interior Design*, Routledge, 1997

William Jackson Bean, *Trees and Shrubs Hardy in the British Isles*, Murray, 1916

John Dransfield and Nathalie W. Uhl, *Genera Palmarum: The Evolution and Classification of Palms*, International Palm Society, 2014

A. F. Entleutner, *Eine Promenade durch die Anlagen und Gärten des climatischen Curortes Meran*, S. Pötzelberger's Buchhandlung, 1886

Martin Gibbons, *Palms: The Illustrated Identifier to Over 100 Palm Species*, Apple Press, 2000

Martin Gibbons and Toby Spanner, *Trachycarpus in the wild and in cultivation*, The Plantsman: New Series, Vol. 12, Issue 2, Royal Horticultural Society, 2003

Dawn Jacobsen, *Chinoiserie*, Phaidon Press Limited, 1993

Owen Jones, *The Grammar of Ornament*, Bernard Quaritch, 1868

Paula von Kohlhaupt, *Kleine Meraner Flora*, Verlagsanstalt Athesia, 1974

Kunst und Kur (exhibition catalog), Kunst Meran Merano Arte, Folio Verlag, 2001

Ernst Wolfgang Mick (ed.), *Hauptwerke des Deutschen Tapetenmuseums in Kassel*, 1981

Steven Parissien, *Interiors: The Home Since 1700*, Laurence King Publishing, 2008

John Pile, *A History of Interior Design*, Laurence King Publishing, 2009

Jim Reynolds, *Palm Trees Shivering in a Surrey Shrubbery: A History of Subtropical Gardening*, Journal of the International Palm Society, Vol. 41 Issue 2, 1999

Paul Lee Riffle and Paul Craft, *An Encyclopedia of Cultivated Palms*, Timber Press, 2003

Matthias Schirren, *Bruno Taut: Alpine Architektur: Eine Utopie*, Prestel, 2004

Benjamin Schmidt, *Inventing Exoticism: Geography, Globalism, and Europe's Early Modern World*, University of Pennsylvania Press, 2015

Victor Segalen, *Essay on Exoticism: An Aesthetics of Diversity*, Duke University Press, 2002

Susanne Stacher and Christoph Hölz, *Dreamland Alps: Utopische Projekte und Projektionen in den Alpen*, Archiv für Baukunst, 2014

Mario Stähler and Tobias W. Spanner, *Winterharte Palmen*, Medemia, 2007

David Squire, *Palms and Cycads: A Complete Guide to Selecting, Growing and Propagating*, Chicago Review Press, 2007

Francoise Teynac, Pierre Nolot, and Jean-Denis Vivien, *Le Monde du papier peint*, Berger-Levrault, 1981

Tropicomania (exhibition catalog), Betonsalon, 2012

**Palm Tree Studies
in South Tyrol and Beyond
Nanna Debois Buhl**

Design: Anni's
Copy editing: Marcella Durand
Print: Ediprima srl, Piacenza
2nd edition: 500
Reprint: 2017

Humboldt Books
via San Marco 33
20121 Milano Italy
www.humboldtbooks.com

ISBN 978-88-99385-07-1

Published on the occasion of the public art exhibition
Art & Nature 2016 Walking With Senses
Merano Spring Festival, Merano, Italy, March 24 – June 5, 2016
Curated by BAU
Commissioned by Municipality of Merano and Merano Tourist Office
Produced by Kunst Meran Merano Arte

Images on middle pages:
Photograms of *Trachycarpus fortunei* plant parts collected in Merano

Archival images:
Design Museum Denmark / Library
The Historical Archive of the City of Merano
Kunst Meran Merano Arte
Library of the Natural History Museum of Denmark
Touriseum Collection - South Tyrol Museum of Tourism
and other sources

Thanks:
BAU and Laura Lovatel
The Gardens of Trauttmansdorff Castle
Joanna Banham, Dorte & Jimmy Buhl, Marcella Durand, Hanne Espersen, Nils Frederiksen, Sara Fruelund, Patrick Gasser, Otto Huber, Astrid Kruse Jensen, Alva Debois Juul, Jesper Juul, Otto Debois Juul, Henning Knudsen, Karin Kompatscher, Nadia Marconi, Karin Maringgele, Sidsel Nelund, Karin Roner, Magdalene Schmidt, Susanne Stacher, Herta Torggler, Anni Vestergaard, Anette Væring, Thomas Wilhalm

Nanna Debois Buhl is a visual artist who lives and works in Copenhagen and New York. She participated in The Whitney Museum's Independent Study Program, New York (2008-09), and received her MFA from The Royal Danish Academy of Fine Arts (2006). Her practice is a continuous investigation of historical and cultural knowledge through botany, animal life, imagery, and architectural components.